SEEING AND SAVORING JESUS CHRIST

SEEING AND SAVORING
JESUS CHRIST

STUDY GUIDE DEVELOPED BY DESIRING GOD

CROSSWAY BOOKS
WHEATON, ILLINOIS

Seeing and Savoring Jesus Christ Study Guide

Copyright © 2008 by Desiring God Foundation

Published by Crossway Books
        a publishing ministry of Good News Publishers
        1300 Crescent Street
        Wheaton, Illinois 60187

This study guide is based on and is a companion to *Seeing and Savoring Jesus Christ* by John Piper (Crossway Books, 2004).

Cover design: Amy Bristow

Cover photo: Josh Dennis

First printing, 2008

Printed in the United States of America

Scripture quotations are taken from *The Holy Bible: English Standard Version*®. Copyright © 2001 by Crossway Bibles, a publishing ministry of Good News Publishers. Used by permission. All rights reserved.

ISBN 978-1-4335-0255-2

BP		16	15	14	13	12	11	10	09	08
14	13	12	11	10	9	8	7	6	5	4	3	2	1

CONTENTS

INTRODUCTION TO THIS STUDY GUIDE

IF SOMEONE WERE TO ASK YOU to describe the greatest problems in the world today, what would you say? War? Poverty? Global warming? In the second letter to the Corinthians, the apostle Paul describes one of the central problems facing humanity in every age. "The god of this world has blinded the minds of the unbelievers, to keep them from seeing the light of the gospel of the glory of Christ, who is the image of God" (2 Corinthians 4:4). One of the greatest problems in the universe is a sight problem. Human beings do not see Christ for who he is. Even those who have caught a glimpse of him do not see perfectly. As Paul says elsewhere, "We see in a mirror dimly" (1 Corinthians 13:12).

So we must see him. But what does this mean? How do you see a person who is not physically present to behold? Where do you look for him? The question becomes more complicated by the fact that in Jesus' own day, there were many who saw him who did not truly *see* him. Concerning them, he said, "Seeing they do not see" (Matthew 13:13). What does this cryptic statement mean?

Jesus is not the only one to offer puzzling statements about seeing him. In 2 Corinthians 3:18 Paul celebrates the fact that "we all, with unveiled face, *beholding the glory of the Lord*, are being transformed into the same image. . . ." But two chapters later he says, "We walk by faith, *not by sight*" (2 Corinthians 5:7). So which is it: do we behold the glory of the Lord, or do we walk by faith, not by sight? Finally, the Bible exhorts us to "Taste and see that the LORD is good!" (Psalm 34:8). But what does it mean to *taste and see* that the Lord is good? Or, to say it another way, what does it mean to see and savor Jesus Christ?

The aim of this study guide is to unpack the meaning and significance of seeing and savoring Jesus Christ. But our goal goes beyond mere explanation. Our hope is not only that people will understand what we mean when we call everyone to see and savor Jesus Christ, but that they will actually answer the call and behold and delight in him above all things. Indeed, our prayer is that this study guide and DVD would be used by God to open the eyes and awaken the hearts of thousands to the truth and beauty of Jesus Christ in the gospel.

This study guide is designed to be used in an eight-session,[1] guided group study that focuses on the *Seeing and Savoring Jesus Christ* DVD Set.[2] After an introductory lesson, each subsequent lesson examines one thirty-minute session[3] from the *Seeing and Savoring Jesus Christ* DVD Set. You, the learner, are encouraged to prepare for the viewing of each DVD session by reading and reflecting upon Scripture, by considering key quotations, and by asking yourself penetrating questions. Your preparatory work for each lesson is marked with the heading "Before You Watch the DVD, Study and Prepare" in Lessons 2-7.

The workload is conveniently divided into five daily (and manageable) assignments. There is also a section suggesting further study. This work is to be completed individually before the group convenes to view the DVD and discuss the material.

> Throughout this study guide, paragraphs printed in a shaded box (like this one) are excerpts from a book written by John Piper or excerpts taken from the Desiring God web site. They are included to supplement the study questions and to summarize key or provocative points.

The second section in Lessons 2-7, entitled "Further Up and Further In," is designed for the learner who wants to explore the concepts and ideas introduced in the lesson in greater detail. This section is not required but will deepen your understanding of the material. This section will provide the opportunity to apply what you are learning through meditation on passages of Scripture in order to see and savor Jesus. To aid you in your meditation, you will also read through *Seeing and Savoring Jesus Christ* by John Piper (Wheaton, IL: Crossway Books, 2004). This book is available for free online at www.desiringGod.org in the Online Books section of the Resource Library. You are also welcome to purchase a copy of the book from Desiring God.

The third section in Lessons 2-7, entitled "While You Watch the DVD, Take Notes," is to be completed as the DVD is playing. This section includes fill-in-the-blanks and leaves space for note-taking. You are encouraged to engage with the DVD by filling in the appropriate blanks and writing down other notes that will aid you in the group discussion.

The fourth section in each normal lesson is "After You Watch the DVD, Discuss What You've Learned." Three discussion questions are provided to guide and focus the conversation. You may record, in the spaces provided, notes that will help you contribute to the conversation. Or you may use this space to record things from the discussion that you want to remember.

The fifth and final section is an application section: "After You Discuss, Make Application." You will be challenged to record a "take-away point" and to engage in a certain activity that is a fitting response to the content presented in the lesson.

Group leaders will want to find the Leader's Guide, included at the end of this study guide, immediately.

Life transformation will only occur by the grace of God. Therefore, we highly encourage you to seek the Lord in prayer throughout the learning process. Pray that God would open your eyes to see wonderful things in his Word. Pray that he would grant you the insight and concentration you need in order to get the most from this resource. Pray that God would cause you to not merely understand the truth but also to rejoice in it. And pray that the discussion in your group would be mutually encouraging and edifying. We've included objectives at the beginning of each lesson. These objectives won't be realized without the gracious work of God through prayer.

NOTES

1. While this study guide is ideally suited for an eight-session study, it is possible to complete it in six sessions. The Leader's Guide at the end of this study guide contains a note on one way to complete this study in six weeks. The six-session option may be well-suited for groups that are already familiar with each other or that only have six weeks to complete the study.

2. Although this resource is designed to be used in a group setting, it can also be used by the independent learner. Such learners would have to decide for themselves how to use this resource in the most beneficial way. We would suggest doing everything but the group discussion, if possible.

3. Thirty minutes is only an approximation. Some sessions are longer; others are shorter.

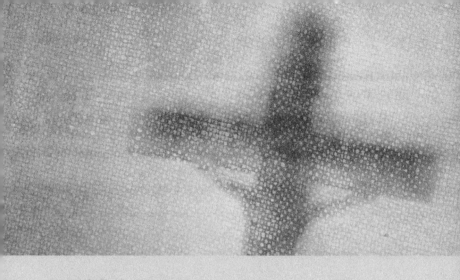

LESSON 1
INTRODUCTION TO *SEEING AND SAVORING JESUS CHRIST*

LESSON OBJECTIVES

It is our prayer that after you have finished this lesson . . .

> You will begin to reflect on the worth and value of Jesus Christ.

> Your curiosity would be roused, and questions would begin to come to mind.

> You will be eager to see and savor more of Jesus Christ in the Word of God.

ABOUT YOURSELF

1) What is your name?

2) Tell the group something about yourself that they probably don't already know.

3) What are you hoping to learn from this study?

A PREVIEW OF *SEEING AND SAVORING JESUS CHRIST*

1) How important is it that Christians learn to see and savor Jesus Christ? What is at stake in seeing and savoring him? Is it possible to see him without savoring him? Explain your answer.

2) What do you love about Jesus Christ? Make a list of attributes or qualities that cause you to treasure Christ. Include biblical stories that display these qualities. Discuss one or two with the group.

His love, mercy, understanding
unfailable truth,

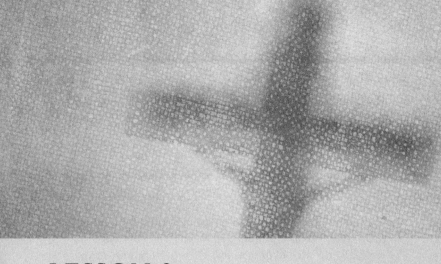

LESSON 2
WHAT DOES IT MEAN TO SEE AND SAVOR JESUS CHRIST?
A Companion Study to the Seeing and Savoring Jesus Christ DVD, Session 1

LESSON OBJECTIVES
It is our prayer that after you have finished this lesson . . .

> You will understand the difference between physical sight and spiritual sight.

> You will grasp the relationship between faith and spiritual sight.

> You will grow in your conviction that the gospel is true and beautiful.

BEFORE YOU WATCH THE DVD, STUDY AND PREPARE

DAY 1: "WE WISH TO SEE JESUS"
The central aim of this study guide is to enable people to see Jesus Christ clearly. The fact that you are participating in this book study indicates that you desire to see him. You are not the first. The

SEEING AND SAVORING JESUS CHRIST

Gospel of John records one example of some people who desired to see Jesus.

Read the following passage.

JOHN 12:20-26

> ^{20} *Now among those who went up to worship at the feast were some Greeks.* ^{21} *So these came to Philip, who was from Bethsaida in Galilee, and asked him, "Sir, we wish to see Jesus."* ^{22} *Philip went and told Andrew; Andrew and Philip went and told Jesus.* ^{23} *And Jesus answered them, "The hour has come for the Son of Man to be glorified.* ^{24} *Truly, truly, I say to you, unless a grain of wheat falls into the earth and dies, it remains alone; but if it dies, it bears much fruit.* ^{25} *Whoever loves his life loses it, and whoever hates his life in this world will keep it for eternal life.* ^{26} *If anyone serves me, he must follow me; and where I am, there will my servant be also. If anyone serves me, the Father will honor him."*

QUESTION 1: How does Jesus respond to the request from the Greeks? In your mind, does this response adequately answer their desire? Why or why not?

But there is one more most crucial thing to say about what sustains us in the path of sacrifice and self-denial. Namely this, and I end with it: Jesus took this path of suffering and death to this destination of glory so that he might become not only our *example* in dying, but, more importantly, our *substitute* in dying. Jesus suffered and died to give us both *pattern* and, more importantly, *pardon*. And the pardon precedes and enables the pattern. We cannot follow the pattern of Jesus' suffering without being freed from God's wrath and our guilt and fear and selfishness. And we are freed from these not by his pattern, but by his pardon. Not by his being our example, but by his being our substitute.

When Jesus died, he didn't just die *before* us—to copy—but *for* us—to trust in. The Good Shepherd laid down his life *for* the sheep—in their place (John 10:11, 15). There must be salvation *by* Jesus before there can be imitation *of* Jesus. There must be justification on the basis of Jesus' death, before there can be sanctification by means of Jesus' power.[1]

QUESTION 2: What is the connection between Jesus being glorified (verse 23), a grain of wheat dying (verse 24), and the obligation of Jesus' servants (verse 26)? How do these three provide a sufficient answer to the request of the Greeks to see Jesus?

DAY 2: TWO TYPES OF SEEING

When we say that we desire to "see" Jesus Christ, it is not always clear what we mean. The Bible teaches that there is more than one kind of "seeing."

Study the following passage.

MATTHEW 13:13-16

> [13] *"This is why I speak to them in parables, because seeing they do not see, and hearing they do not hear, nor do they understand.* [14] *Indeed, in their case the prophecy of Isaiah is fulfilled that says: 'You will indeed hear but never understand, and you will indeed see but never perceive.* [15] *For this people's heart has grown dull, and with their ears they can barely hear, and their eyes they have closed, lest they should see with their eyes and hear with their ears and understand with their heart and turn, and I would heal them.'* [16] *But blessed are your eyes, for they see, and your ears, for they hear."*

QUESTION 3: What is meant by the phrase "seeing they do not see"? In what sense do these people see? In what sense do they not see? Distinguish between these two types of seeing.

Jesus is not the only one who teaches that there are two types of seeing.

Examine the following passage.

EPHESIANS 1:15-19

> [15] *For this reason, because I have heard of your faith in the Lord Jesus and your love toward all the saints,* [16] *I do not cease to give thanks for you, remembering you in my prayers,* [17] *that the God of our Lord Jesus Christ, the Father of glory, may give you a spirit of wisdom and of revelation in the knowledge of him,* [18] *having the eyes of your hearts enlightened, that you may know what is the hope to which he has called you, what are the riches of his glorious inheritance in the saints,* [19] *and what is the*

immeasurable greatness of his power toward us who believe, according to the working of his great might.

QUESTION 4: In this passage, what do the eyes of the heart see? What does Paul mean by "the eyes of your hearts"? How do these eyes differ from the eyes of your head? Is it possible to see something with the eyes of your head but not see it with the eyes of your heart? Provide an example.

What then is this seeing with the eyes of the heart? It is a spiritual perception of the truth and beauty and worth of Christ for what they really are. To use the words of Jonathan Edwards, it is "a true sense of the divine excellency of the things revealed in the Word of God, and a conviction of the truth and reality of them thence arising." The key word here is "sense." The person who sees with the eyes of the heart "does not merely rationally believe that God is glorious, but he has a *sense* of the gloriousness of God in his heart. There is not only a rational belief that God is holy, and that holiness is a good thing, but there is a sense of the loveliness of God's holiness."[2]

DAY 3: FAITH AND SIGHT
Study 2 Corinthians 3:18 and 2 Corinthians 4:16-18.

2 CORINTHIANS 3:18

18 And we all, with unveiled face, beholding the glory of the Lord, are being transformed into the same image from one degree of glory to another. For this comes from the Lord who is the Spirit.

2 CORINTHIANS 4:16-18

16 So we do not lose heart. Though our outer nature is wasting away, our inner self is being renewed day by day. 17 For this light momentary affliction is preparing for us an eternal weight of glory beyond all comparison, 18 as we look not to the things that are seen but to the things that are unseen. For the things that are seen are transient, but the things that are unseen are eternal.

QUESTION 5: Write down six total observations about spiritual sight from these passages. What is the result of seeing Christ in each passage?

By seeing the glory of Christ in the gospel we are changed. In what way? Not first externally, but first internally. What is this internal change that comes from "beholding the glory of the Lord"?

It is the awakening of joy in Christ himself, and all that God is for us in him. It is the awakening of a new taste for spiritual reality centering in Christ. It is the capacity for a new sweetness and a new enjoyment of the glory of God in the

Word of God. Therefore, nothing is more important for us in life than to "behold the glory of the Lord."[3]

Read 2 Corinthians 5:7 and 1 Peter 1:8-9.

2 CORINTHIANS 5:7

For we walk by faith, not by sight.

1 PETER 1:8-9

[8] *Though you have not seen him, you love him. Though you do not now see him, you believe in him and rejoice with joy that is inexpressible and filled with glory,* [9] *obtaining the outcome of your faith, the salvation of your souls.*

QUESTION 6: Describe the relationship between faith and sight. How does faith relate to physical sight? How does it relate to seeing with the eyes of the heart? Which type of sight do Paul and Peter refer to in these texts?

DAY 4: HOW CAN WE BE SURE?

Many people struggle to believe that the picture of Jesus presented in the Bible is true. There are different approaches to answering these doubts.

But how can you be sure that the biblical portrait of Jesus is true? People take two paths in search of solid ground under the feet of faith. One is the path of painstaking historical research to test the authenticity of the historical records. I followed this path during my formative years in seminary and graduate school and college teaching. . . .

But now I am a pastor rather than a college teacher. I still value the path of scholarly historical research. In fact, I lean on it often. However, I am immediately aware now that the vast majority of people in the world will never have the time or the tools to trace out all the evidences for the historical reliability of the New Testament. If Jesus is the Son of God, if he died for our sins and rose from the dead, and if God meant for people, two thousand years later, to have a well-founded faith, then there must be another path to know the real Jesus, other than by rigorous, academic, historical research.[4]

QUESTION 7: How would you counsel a person who struggles to believe that the biblical portrait of Jesus is true? How would you respond if he or she felt that he or she needed to be a biblical scholar in order to have genuine assurance?

In the quotation above, John Piper mentions two paths in the search for solid ground under the feet of faith. Here is the second.

There is another path. It's the path I have followed in this book. It starts with the conviction that divine truth can be self-authenticating. In fact, it would seem strange if God revealed himself in his Son Jesus Christ and inspired the record of that revelation in the Bible, but did not provide a way for ordinary people to know it. Stated most simply, the common path to sure knowledge of the real Jesus is this: Jesus, as he is revealed in the Bible, has a glory—an excellence, a spiritual beauty—that can be seen as self-evidently true. It is like seeing the sun and knowing that it is light and not dark, or like tasting honey and knowing that it is sweet and not sour. There is no long chain of reasoning from premises to conclusions. There is a direct apprehension that this person is true and his glory is the glory of God.[5]

QUESTION 8: How does John Piper help ordinary people come to a strong conviction of the truth of the gospel? How can this path to solid ground under the feet of faith be an encouragement to missionaries who work among unreached people groups or to you in personal evangelism?

The practical effect of this path is that I do not ask you to pray for a special whisper from God to decide if Jesus is real. Rather I ask you to look at the Jesus of the Bible. Look at him. Don't close your eyes and hope for a word of confirmation. Keep your eyes open and fill them with the full portrait of Jesus provided in the Bible. If you come to trust

Jesus Christ as Lord and God, it will be because you see in him a divine glory and excellence that simply is what it is—true.[6]

DAY 5: TASTE AND SEE

It is abundantly clear from Scripture and from experience that not everyone who sees Jesus embraces him as their Savior, Lord, and Treasure. Many reject him. Paul describes the result of his proclamation of the gospel to the church at Corinth.

Study the following passage.

1 CORINTHIANS 1:22-24

22 For Jews demand signs and Greeks seek wisdom, 23 but we preach Christ crucified, a stumbling block to Jews and folly to Gentiles, 24 but to those who are called, both Jews and Greeks, Christ the power of God and the wisdom of God.

QUESTION 9: According to this text, how do Jews and Greeks respond to the gospel of Christ crucified? Do all Jews and Greeks respond this way? What is the difference between those who respond positively and those who respond negatively?

Notice two kinds of "calls" implied in this text.

First, the preaching of Paul goes out to all, both Jews and Greeks. This is the general call of the gospel. It offers salvation to all who will believe on the crucified Christ. But by and large it falls on unreceptive ears and is called foolishness.

But then, secondly, Paul refers to another kind of call. He says that among those who hear there are some who are "called" in such a way that they no longer regard the cross as foolishness but as the wisdom and power of God. What else can this call be but the irresistible call of God out of darkness into the light of God?[7]

To this point in the lesson, we have focused mainly on "seeing." The last question will connect seeing to savoring.

Examine Psalm 34:8 and 1 Peter 2:2-3.

PSALM 34:8

[8] *Oh, taste and see that the LORD is good! Blessed is the man who takes refuge in him!*

1 PETER 2:2-3

[2] *Like newborn infants, long for the pure spiritual milk, that by it you may grow up into salvation—* [3] *if indeed you have tasted that the Lord is good.*

QUESTION 10: In your mind, is seeing (in the sense described in this lesson) fundamentally different from savoring? What, if any, is the difference between seeing and savoring? How would you explain "savoring Jesus Christ" to someone who had never heard of this concept before?

There is a difference between having a rational judgment that honey is sweet, and having a sense of its sweetness. A man may have the former, that knows not how honey tastes; but a man cannot have the latter unless he has an idea of the taste of honey in his mind. So there is a difference between believing that a person is beautiful, and having a sense of his beauty. The former may be obtained by hearsay, but the latter only by seeing the countenance. There is a wide difference between mere speculative rational judging any thing to be excellent, and having a sense of its sweetness and beauty. The former rests only in the head, speculation only is concerned in it; but the heart is concerned in the latter. When the heart is sensible of the beauty and amiableness of a thing, it necessarily feels pleasure in the apprehension. It is implied in a person's being heartily sensible of the loveliness of a thing, that the idea of it is sweet and pleasant to his soul; which is a far different thing from having a rational opinion that it is excellent.[8]

FURTHER UP AND FURTHER IN

As noted in the introduction, each lesson in this study guide provides the opportunity for you to apply what you've been learning to your own study of Scripture. In this section, you will be given a number of biblical texts for reflection and meditation. We encourage you to think, reflect, and pray through these texts with a view to seeing and savoring Jesus Christ. As you read, ask yourself these questions:

> What do you learn about Jesus in each passage?
> What qualities or attributes of Jesus are prominent?
> What is emphasized about who he is or what he's done or why he is worthy to be savored?

Record your reflections in the space provided. After you have done your own reflection, you will read a chapter in *Seeing and Savoring Jesus Christ* in which John Piper reflects on similar biblical passages and themes. After you have read the chapter, we encourage you to add to your own reflections or to write a prayer that expresses the substance of your meditation. Our hope is that by reflecting on the biblical text and reading through the meditations of John Piper, you will grow in your ability to see and savor Jesus Christ for yourself.

REFLECTION #1: THE ULTIMATE AIM OF JESUS CHRIST
Meditate on the following biblical texts in your own Bible:
- John 17:1-5, 24-26
- Romans 1:18-25
- 2 Corinthians 3:18-4:6

Read "A Word to the Reader" and Chapter 1, "Seeing and Savoring the Glory of God," in *Seeing and Savoring Jesus Christ.*

REFLECTION #2: THE DEITY OF JESUS CHRIST
Meditate on the following biblical texts in your own Bible:
- Isaiah 44:6
- John 1:1-18
- Hebrews 1:1-3
- Revelation 1:8
- Revelation 22:12-13

Read Chapter 2, "Jesus Is the Glory of God," in *Seeing and Savoring Jesus Christ*.

WHILE YOU WATCH THE DVD, TAKE NOTES
According to John Piper, what are the two kinds of sight?

How does John Piper define spiritual sight?

_____ _____ we are changed into _____. _____ is _____.

True or False: The surest kind of knowledge of God comes from a long chain of rational arguments. _____

A little child may look at a _____ and prefer a _____ _____.

AFTER YOU WATCH THE DVD, DISCUSS WHAT YOU'VE LEARNED

1) Discuss the nature of spiritual sight. How does it relate to physical sight? What do we see with the eyes of our heart?

2) What is the main point that John Piper derives from the lengthy quote from Jonathan Edwards? How might this truth give us great confidence in evangelism?

3) Why is it important that we stress both seeing and savoring? What aspect of Christian faith does "savoring" emphasize?

AFTER YOU DISCUSS, MAKE APPLICATION

1) What was the most meaningful part of this lesson for you? Was there a sentence, concept, or idea that really struck you? Why? Record your thoughts in the space below.

2) Read slowly through Ephesians 1:15-23. Pray through this passage for yourself and for the others in your

group. Meditate on each of the phrases in this prayer. Record your reflections below.

NOTES

1. Excerpt taken from an online sermon at the Desiring God web site entitled, "Where I Am There Will My Servant Be: A Call to Treasure Christ Together." Throughout this study guide, articles and sermons at the Desiring God web site (www.desiringGod.org) may be found by performing a title search on the home page.

2. Excerpt taken from *When I Don't Desire God*, pages 67-68.

3. Excerpt taken from *When I Don't Desire God*, page 66.

4. Excerpt taken from *Seeing and Savoring Jesus Christ*, pages 118-119.

5. Excerpt taken from *Seeing and Savoring Jesus Christ*, pages 119-120.

6. Excerpt taken from *Seeing and Savoring Jesus Christ*, page 121.

7. Excerpt taken from an online article at the Desiring God web site en-titled, "What We Believe About the Five Points of Calvinism."

8. Excerpt taken from a sermon by Jonathan Edwards entitled "A Divine and Supernatural Light." This sermon may be found in *The Works of Jonathan Edwards*, Vol. 2 (Peabody, MA: Hendrickson, 1998).

LESSON 3
SEEING AND SAVORING JESUS CHRIST IN THE GOSPEL

A Companion Study to the Seeing and Savoring Jesus Christ DVD, Session 2

LESSON OBJECTIVES

It is our prayer that after you have finished this lesson . . .

> You will grasp the centrality of the gospel for seeing and savoring Jesus Christ.

> You will embrace the terrible wonder of the love of God in the cross.

> You will more fully treasure Christ for his wrath-bearing, sin-atoning, and devil-defeating work.

BEFORE YOU WATCH THE DVD, STUDY AND PREPARE

DAY 1: WHERE IS JESUS?

In the last lesson you learned that the Bible places great emphasis on seeing with the eyes of the heart. You also learned that when we see with spiritual eyes, we see the glory and excellency of Jesus

Christ. But Christ is no longer bodily present with us. So where do we look if we want to see him?

QUESTION 1: Where do we look if we want to see Jesus? Make a list of places where Jesus may be spiritually seen.

Examine the following passage.

2 CORINTHIANS 4:4-6

[4] *In their case the god of this world has blinded the minds of the unbelievers, to keep them from seeing the light of the gospel of the glory of Christ, who is the image of God.* [5] *For what we proclaim is not ourselves, but Jesus Christ as Lord, with ourselves as your servants for Jesus' sake.* [6] *For God, who said, "Let light shine out of darkness," has shone in our hearts to give the light of the knowledge of the glory of God in the face of Jesus Christ.*

QUESTION 2: What is Satan's goal in this passage? What is God's response? Underline similar words and phrases in verse 4 and verse 6. What does this passage teach us regarding where we can look to see the glory of Christ?

The spiritual beauty of Christ is Christ-in-action—Christ loving, and Christ touching lepers, and Christ blessing children, and healing the crippled, and raising the dead, and commanding demons, and teaching with unrivaled authority, and silencing the skeptics, and rebuking his disciples, and predicting the details of his death, and setting his face like flint toward Jerusalem, and weeping over the city, and silent before his accusers, and meekly sovereign over Pilate ("You would have no authority over me at all unless it had been given you from above," John 19:11), and crucified, and praying for his enemies, and forgiving a thief, and caring for his mother while in agony, and giving up his spirit in death, and rising from the dead—"No one takes [my life] from me, but I lay it down of my own accord. I have authority to lay it down, and I have authority to take it up again" (John 10:18). Such is the glory of Christ.[1]

DAY 2: SEEING AND HEARING

Read Romans 10:17, Galatians 3:2, and 1 Samuel 3:21.

ROMANS 10:17

So faith comes from hearing, and hearing through the word of Christ.

GALATIANS 3:2

Let me ask you only this: Did you receive the Spirit by works of the law or by hearing with faith?

1 SAMUEL 3:21

And the LORD appeared again at Shiloh, for the LORD revealed himself to Samuel at Shiloh by the word of the LORD.

QUESTION 3: What is the relationship between seeing Christ spiritually and hearing that leads to faith? How does 1 Samuel 3:21 bridge the gap between seeing and hearing?

The relationship between the Word of God and the glory of God is remarkable, and we should grasp it firmly. God ordained that spiritual *seeing* should happen mainly through *hearing*. Christ is not visually present for us to see. He is presented today in the Word of God, especially the gospel. Paul said, "Faith comes from hearing, and hearing through the word of Christ" (Rom. 10:17). But we know from 2 Corinthians 4:4 that faith springs from "seeing the light of the gospel of the glory of Christ." Therefore we can say that seeing the glory of Christ is what happens in the heart when the hearing of the gospel is made effective by the Spirit. That is, when, through the gospel, the omnipotent, creative voice of God says, "Let light shine in the darkness of this heart," the gospel gives rise to faith. When hearing, by grace, produces seeing, it produces faith.[2]

It is possible to misunderstand the nature of spiritual sight. Some people may conclude that there is no relation whatsoever between seeing Christ spiritually and the objective Word of God. Indeed, some may even infer that spiritual sight goes beyond what is written in the Bible. Jonathan Edwards helpfully clarifies this point.

This spiritual light is not the suggesting of any new truths, or propositions not contained in the Word of God. This suggesting of new truths or doctrines to the mind, independently of any antecedent revelation of those propositions, either in word or writing, is inspiration; such as the prophets and apostles had, and such as some enthusiasts pretend to. But this spiritual light that I am speaking of, is quite a different thing from inspiration: it reveals no new doctrine, it suggests no new proposition to the mind, it teaches no new thing of God, or Christ, or another world, not taught in the Bible; but only gives a due apprehension of those things that are taught in the Word of God.[3]

QUESTION 4: How does Edwards connect the spiritual light that shines in the soul to the truth of the Word of God? Does this spiritual sight go beyond what is written in Scripture?

DAY 3: SEEING CHRIST IN THE GOSPEL

In the last section you saw that the preeminent place where Christ is seen with the eyes of the heart is the gospel. The glory of Christ shines most brightly in and through the good news of his life, death, and resurrection. Thus, if we want to see Jesus, we would do well to look at what he accomplished for us in his sacrificial death and victorious resurrection.

Study the following passage.

GALATIANS 3:10-14

> [10] For all who rely on works of the law are under a curse; for it is written, "Cursed be everyone who does not abide by all things written in the Book of the Law, and do them." [11] Now it is evident that no one is justified before God by the law, for "The righteous shall live by faith." [12] But the law is not of faith, rather "The one who does them shall live by them." [13] Christ redeemed us from the curse of the law by becoming a curse for us—for it is written, "Cursed is everyone who is hanged on a tree"— [14] so that in Christ Jesus the blessing of Abraham might come to the Gentiles, so that we might receive the promised Spirit through faith.

QUESTION 5: What is the chief problem faced by human beings in this text? How does the cross of Christ solve this problem? What is the result of Christ's sacrifice on our behalf?

There is a holy curse hanging over all sin. Not to punish would be unjust. The demeaning of God would be endorsed. A lie would reign at the core of reality. Therefore, God says, "Cursed be everyone who does not abide by all things written in the Book of the Law, and do them" (Galatians 3:10; Deuteronomy 27:26).

But the love of God does not rest with the curse that hangs over all sinful humanity. He is not content to show wrath, no matter how holy it is. Therefore God sends his own Son to absorb his wrath and bear the curse for all who trust him. "Christ redeemed us from the curse of the law by becoming a curse for us" (Galatians 3:13).[4]

The glory of Christ in the gospel was foretold centuries before Jesus was born. Isaiah 53 testifies to the Suffering Servant who would redeem his people.

Read the following passage.

ISAIAH 53

¹ *Who has believed what he has heard from us? And to whom has the arm of the* LORD *been revealed?* ² *For he grew up before him like a young plant, and like a root out of dry ground; he had no form or majesty that we should look at him, and no beauty that we should desire him.* ³ *He was despised and rejected by men; a man of sorrows, and acquainted with grief; and as one from whom men hide their faces he was despised, and we esteemed him not.* ⁴ *Surely he has borne our griefs and carried our sorrows; yet we esteemed him stricken, smitten by God, and afflicted.* ⁵ *But he was wounded for our transgressions; he was crushed for our iniquities; upon him was the chastisement that brought us peace, and with his stripes we are healed.* ⁶ *All we like sheep have gone astray; we have turned—every one—to his own way; and the* LORD *has laid on him the iniquity of us all.* ⁷ *He was oppressed, and he was afflicted, yet he opened not his mouth; like a lamb that is led to the slaughter, and like a sheep that before its shearers is silent, so he opened not his mouth.* ⁸ *By oppression and judgment he was taken away; and as for his generation, who considered that he was cut off out of the land of the living, stricken for the transgression of my people?* ⁹ *And they made his grave with the wicked and with a rich man in his death, although he had done no violence, and there was no deceit in his mouth.* ¹⁰ *Yet it was the will of the* LORD *to crush him; he has put him to grief; when his soul makes an offering for sin, he shall see his offspring; he shall prolong his days; the will of the* LORD *shall prosper in his hand.* ¹¹ *Out of the anguish of his soul he shall see and be satisfied; by his knowledge shall the righteous one, my servant, make many to be accounted righteous, and he shall bear their iniquities.* ¹² *Therefore I will divide him a portion with the many, and he shall divide the spoil with the strong, because he poured out his soul to death and was*

numbered with the transgressors; yet he bore the sin of many,
and makes intercession for the transgressors.

The book of 1 Peter contains considerable reflection on Isaiah's prophecy.

Examine the following passage.

1 PETER 2:21-25

> [21] *For to this you have been called, because Christ also suffered for you, leaving you an example, so that you might follow in his steps.* [22] *He committed no sin, neither was deceit found in his mouth.* [23] *When he was reviled, he did not revile in return; when he suffered, he did not threaten, but continued entrusting himself to him who judges justly.* [24] *He himself bore our sins in his body on the tree, that we might die to sin and live to righteousness. By his wounds you have been healed.* [25] *For you were straying like sheep, but have now returned to the Shepherd and Overseer of your souls.*

QUESTION 6: Underline common words and phrases between Isaiah 53 and 1 Peter 2. What is the central thrust of these passages? How do these passages display the glory of Christ to you?

Oh, that we might worship the terrible wonder of the love of God! It is not sentimental. It is not simple. For our sake God did the impossible: He poured out his wrath on his own Son—the one whose submission made him infinitely unworthy to receive it. Yet the Son's very willingness to receive it was precious in God's sight. The wrath-bearer was infinitely loved.[5]

DAY 4: FREEING FROM DEATH AND DESTROYING THE DEVIL

The wrath of God against human sin was not the only obstacle that hindered us from enjoying God forever.

Study Hebrews 2:14-15, 1 John 3:8, and Colossians 2:13-15.

HEBREWS 2:14-15

[14] *Since therefore the children share in flesh and blood, he himself likewise partook of the same things, that through death he might destroy the one who has the power of death, that is, the devil,* [15] *and deliver all those who through fear of death were subject to lifelong slavery.*

1 JOHN 3:8

[8] *Whoever makes a practice of sinning is of the devil, for the devil has been sinning from the beginning. The reason the Son of God appeared was to destroy the works of the devil.*

COLOSSIANS 2:13-15

[13] *And you, who were dead in your trespasses and the uncircumcision of your flesh, God made alive together with him, having forgiven us all our trespasses,* [14] *by canceling the record of debt that stood against us with its legal demands. This he set aside, nailing it to the cross.* [15] *He disarmed the rulers and authorities and put them to open shame, by triumphing over them in him.*

QUESTION 7: According to these passages, what did Christ accomplish on the cross? Underline every phrase that refers to this accomplishment.

The death of Jesus was the decisive defeat of "the ruler of this world"—the devil. And as Satan goes, so go all his fallen angels. All of them were dealt a decisive blow of defeat when Christ died.

Not that they were put out of existence. We wrestle with them even now. But they are a defeated foe. We know we have the final victory. It is as though a great dragon has had his head cut off and is thrashing about until he bleeds to death. The battle is won. But we must still be careful of the damage he can do.[6]

QUESTION 8: The texts above teach that Christ disarmed the rulers and authorities and destroyed the works of the devil. What is the weapon that Satan uses to destroy us? How was this weapon taken out of his hand at the cross?

DAY 5: THE LOVE OF GOD IN THE CROSS OF CHRIST

Not only did Christ absorb the wrath of God, bear our sins, and destroy the works of the devil, he also displayed the abundance of his love for helpless sinners.

Study the following passage.

ROMANS 5:6-11

> [6] *For while we were still weak, at the right time Christ died for the ungodly.* [7] *For one will scarcely die for a righteous person—though perhaps for a good person one would dare even to die—* [8] *but God shows his love for us in that while we were still sinners, Christ died for us.* [9] *Since, therefore, we have now been justified by his blood, much more shall we be saved by him from the wrath of God.* [10] *For if while we were enemies we were reconciled to God by the death of his Son, much more, now that we are reconciled, shall we be saved by his life.* [11] *More than that, we also rejoice in God through our Lord Jesus Christ, through whom we have now received reconciliation.*

QUESTION 9: According to this text, what is so shocking about the love of Christ for us? How does the cross of Christ give us great confidence and hope as we approach the future judgment?

The measure of his love for us increases still more when we consider our unworthiness. "Perhaps for a good person one would dare even to die—but God shows his love for us in that *while we were still sinners*, Christ died for us" (Romans 5:7-8). We deserved divine punishment, not divine sacrifice.

I have heard it said, "God didn't die for frogs. So he was responding to our value as humans." This turns grace on its head. We are *worse* off than frogs. They have not sinned. They have not rebelled and treated God with the contempt of being inconsequential in their lives. God did not have to die for frogs. They aren't bad enough. We are. Our debt is so great, only a divine sacrifice could pay it.

There is only one explanation for God's sacrifice for us. It is not us. It is "the riches of his grace" (Ephesians 1:7). It is all free. It is not a response to our worth. It is the overflow of his infinite worth. In fact, that is what divine love is in the end: a passion to enthrall undeserving sinners, at great cost, with what will make us supremely happy forever, namely, his infinite beauty.[7]

The love of God in the cross does not terminate with us. God's love flows from him and returns back to him.

Read 1 Peter 3:18 and Ephesians 2:13.

1 PETER 3:18

For Christ also suffered once for sins, the righteous for the unrighteous, that he might bring us to God.

EPHESIANS 2:13

But now in Christ Jesus you who once were far off have been brought near by the blood of Christ.

QUESTION 10: What is the purpose of the cross in these texts? How does this purpose display the glory of Christ in the gospel? How does this purpose relate to the demonstration of God's love for sinners?

This is the greatest thing Christ died for. "Christ also suffered once for sins, the righteous for the unrighteous, *that he might bring us to God*" (1 Peter 3:18).

Why is this the essence of the good news? Because we were made to experience full and lasting happiness from seeing and savoring the glory of God. If our best joy comes from something less, we are idolaters and God is dishonored. He created us in such a way that his glory is displayed through our joy in it. The gospel of Christ is the good news that at the cost of his Son's life, God has done everything necessary to enthrall us with what will make us eternally and ever-increasingly happy, namely, himself.[8]

FURTHER UP AND FURTHER IN

REFLECTION #1: THE EXCELLENCE OF JESUS CHRIST
Meditate on the following biblical texts in your own Bible:
- Revelation 5
- Matthew 28:18-20
- Matthew 11:28-30

Read Chapter 3, "The Lion and the Lamb," in *Seeing and Savoring Jesus Christ*.

REFLECTION #2: THE GLADNESS OF JESUS CHRIST
Meditate on the following biblical texts in your own Bible:
- John 15:9-11
- Hebrews 12:1-3
- Acts 2:22-31
- Isaiah 53:1-5
- Hebrews 1:6-9

Read Chapter 4, "The Indestructible Joy," in *Seeing and Savoring Jesus Christ*.

REFLECTION #3: THE POWER OF JESUS CHRIST
Meditate on the following biblical texts in your own Bible:
- Psalm 29
- Mark 4:35-41
- Psalm 148
- Luke 7:11-17

Read Chapter 5, "The Waves and Winds Still Know His Voice," in *Seeing and Savoring Jesus Christ*.

WHILE YOU WATCH THE DVD, TAKE NOTES

According to John Piper, what is the main place that we should look to see the glory of Jesus Christ?

The Holy Spirit uses _____ to grant _____ through the _____ of the _____.

What advice does John Piper give to unbelievers who haven't yet experienced spiritual sight?

The four Gospels skip the majority of Jesus' life because:

What is Satan's one weapon that he uses against human beings?

AFTER YOU WATCH THE DVD, DISCUSS WHAT YOU'VE LEARNED

1) Why is it important that we connect seeing and savoring Jesus Christ to the gospel? Why is it dangerous to move away from our Bibles to seek to see his glory elsewhere?

2) Discuss whether God ever gets angry with his children.

3) If Christ defeated the devil in his work on the cross, how do we account for the fact that Satan is still active in the world?

AFTER YOU DISCUSS, MAKE APPLICATION

1) What was the most meaningful part of this lesson for you? Was there a sentence, concept, or idea that really

struck you? Why? Record your thoughts in the space below.

2) In this lesson you learned that spiritual seeing often takes place through hearing the gospel. With the help of another believer, choose a few of the biblical texts covered in this lesson (or others that you know of) and take turns reading the Word of God to each other aloud. If you are unable to find another believer, read these texts out loud to yourself. What do you notice in hearing the texts read aloud that you never noticed before? Record your reflections below.

NOTES

1. Excerpt taken from *God Is the Gospel*, page 66.
2. Excerpt taken from *When I Don't Desire God*, page 65.
3. Excerpt taken from a sermon by Jonathan Edwards entitled "A Divine and Supernatural Light." This sermon may be found in *The Works of Jonathan Edwards*, Vol. 2 (Peabody, MA: Hendrickson, 1998).
4. Excerpt taken from *50 Reasons Why Jesus Came to Die*, page 21.
5. Excerpt taken from *50 Reasons Why Jesus Came to Die*, page 23.
6. Excerpt taken from *50 Reasons Why Jesus Came to Die*, pages 102-103.
7. Excerpt taken from *50 Reasons Why Jesus Came to Die*, page 29.
8. Excerpt taken from *50 Reasons Why Jesus Came to Die*, page 63.

LESSON 4
THE IMPORTANCE OF SEEING AND SAVORING
A Companion Study to the Seeing and Savoring Jesus Christ DVD, Session 3

LESSON OBJECTIVES

It is our prayer that after you have finished this lesson . . .

> You will fully grasp the crucial importance of seeing and savoring Jesus Christ.

> You will grow in your understanding of saving faith.

> You will understand the necessity of a new nature if we are to see and savor Jesus Christ.

BEFORE YOU WATCH THE DVD, STUDY AND PREPARE

DAY 1: SEEING, SAVORING, AND SALVATION

To this point in the study, we have discussed what it means to see and savor. In this lesson, you will reflect on the importance of seeing and savoring. How crucial is it that a person see the glory of Christ with the eyes of the heart?

QUESTION 1: Give three reasons why you think it is crucial that we see and savor Jesus Christ. What is at stake in seeing and savoring?

For John Piper, the fight to see and savor Jesus Christ is absolutely essential. In fact, eternal life depends on it. Listen to John Piper argue for this point.

> A person who has no taste for the enjoyment of Christ will not go to heaven. "If anyone has no love for the Lord, let him be accursed" (1 Cor. 16:22). "Whoever loves father or mother more than me is not worthy of me, and whoever loves son or daughter more than me is not worthy of me" (Matt. 10:37). "Though you have not seen him, you love him. Though you do not now see him, you believe in him and rejoice with joy that is inexpressible and filled with glory" (1 Pet. 1:8). Loving Jesus, not just "deciding" for him or "being committed to him" or affirming all the right doctrines about him, is the mark of a true child of God. Jesus said, "If God were your Father, you would love me" (John 8:42).
>
> Yes, I am assuming that loving Jesus includes the taste of joy in his personhood. I reject the notion that love for Christ is identical to mental or physical acts done in obedience to his Word. When Jesus said, "If you love me, you will keep my commandments" (John 14:15), he was describing the *effect* of love, not the essence of love. First there is love, then there is the effect—obedience. . . . Loving Christ in-

volves delight in his Person. Without this love no one goes to heaven. Therefore there is no more important struggle in the universe than the struggle to see and savor Jesus Christ above all things—the struggle for joy.[1]

John Piper has described this point elsewhere in relation to 2 Corinthians 4:4-6.

The glory of God in the face of Christ—that is, the glory of Christ who is the image of God—is essential to the gospel. It is not marginal or dispensable. Paul calls the gospel "the gospel of the glory of Christ." This glory is what the events of the gospel are designed to reveal. If a person comes to the gospel and sees the events of Good Friday and Easter and believes that they happened and that they can bring some peace of mind, but does not see and savor any of this divine glory, that person does not have saving faith.[2]

QUESTION 2: Interact with these statements by John Piper. Do you agree that seeing and savoring Jesus Christ is necessary for salvation? Can a person be saved who embraces Christ for some of his benefits but does not see and savor the worth and excellency of Jesus Christ? Why or why not?

DAY 2: WHAT IS FAITH?
Examine John 6:35, Hebrews 11:6, and Ephesians 2:8-10.

JOHN 6:35

Jesus said to them, "I am the bread of life; whoever comes to me shall not hunger, and whoever believes in me shall never thirst."

HEBREWS 11:6

And without faith it is impossible to please him, for whoever would draw near to God must believe that he exists and that he rewards those who seek him.

EPHESIANS 2:8-10

[8] For by grace you have been saved through faith. And this is not your own doing; it is the gift of God, [9] not a result of works, so that no one may boast. [10] For we are his workmanship, created in Christ Jesus for good works, which God prepared beforehand, that we should walk in them.

QUESTION 3: From these passages, construct your own definition of faith. What is the essential difference between faith and works? What is the relationship between faith and works? Why is it crucial that salvation be by grace and through faith?

Faith is essential in the human heart if we are to glorify God. God is shown to be glorious when we trust Him, especially in suffering. Faith is seeing and savoring the glory of God in Christ crucified, risen, and reigning for the good of His people (2 Corinthians 4:4-6). This "savoring" means receiving in Christ the superior satisfaction of His promises based on His finished work of atonement (Philippians 3:7-9). Faith is the soul's embrace of all that God is and promises to be for us in Christ (Hebrews 11:1). It honors God by being confident that God will keep His promises to those who set their hope on Him (Romans 4:20-21). Thus faith is future-oriented while resting firmly on the past work of Christ on the Cross and in the resurrection. Faith glorifies God because it magnifies His power, wisdom, grace and faithfulness to work for us the good that we cannot do for ourselves.[3]

Read the following passage.

JOHN 1:12-13

[12] *But to all who did receive him, who believed in his name, he gave the right to become children of God,* [13] *who were born, not of blood nor of the will of the flesh nor of the will of man, but of God.*

QUESTION 4: What do you learn about the nature of believing from this passage? What does it mean to "receive Christ"? Is it possible to receive him for the wrong reasons? If yes, provide examples.

DAY 3: WHAT DOES IT MEAN TO TRUST JESUS?

QUESTION 5: How would you respond to someone who believed in Jesus as rescuer from sin and hell but did not savor him as the supreme treasure of their lives? What counsel or warning would you give to such a person?

> Until the gospel *events* of Good Friday and Easter and the gospel *promises* of justification and eternal life lead you to behold and embrace God *himself* as your highest joy, you have not embraced the gospel of God. You have embraced some of his gifts. You have rejoiced over some of his rewards. You have marveled at some of his miracles. But you have not yet been awakened to why the gifts, the rewards, and the miracles have come. They have come for one great reason: that you might behold forever the glory of God in Christ, and by beholding become the kind of person who delights in God above all things, and by delighting display his supreme beauty and worth with ever-increasing brightness and bliss forever.[4]

QUESTION 6: For each of the following benefits of the gospel, decide whether a new nature is required for someone to desire and embrace it. Explain your decisions.

> a clean conscience
> deliverance from hell
> the beauty of Christ
> solutions to family problems
> fellowship with the Holy Spirit

DAY 4: LET GOODS AND KINDRED GO

Study Matthew 10:37-39 and Luke 14:33.

MATTHEW 10:37-39

37 Whoever loves father or mother more than me is not worthy of me, and whoever loves son or daughter more than me is not worthy of me. 38 And whoever does not take his cross and follow me is not worthy of me. 39 Whoever finds his life will lose it, and whoever loses his life for my sake will find it.

LUKE 14:33

So therefore, any one of you who does not renounce all that he has cannot be my disciple.

QUESTION 7: Do these texts describe a command that is binding upon all Christians or only some Christians? Explain your answer.

QUESTION 8: What is the main point of these texts? How do we reconcile such passages with Jesus' command to "love your neighbor as yourself" (Matt. 22:39)? Do these passages mean that we shouldn't love our families at all?

DAY 5: SELF-ESTEEM VS. INSIGNIFICANCE

One of the most pervasive ideologies in the world is the idea that true happiness comes by increasing your self-esteem. The following excerpt from a pamphlet entitled "My Declaration of Self-Esteem" describes this belief:

> I am me. In all the world, there is no one else exactly like me. Everything that comes out of me is authentically mine because I alone chose it. . . . I own me, and therefore I can engineer me—I am me, and I am OKAY.[5]

QUESTION 9: Do you believe that all human beings desire to have a high self-esteem? Is this a holy desire or a sinful one? Cite Scripture in your answer.

QUESTION 10: In your mind, why are people drawn to visit the Grand Canyon and other natural wonders? Why do people go to musical concerts and sporting events? How might these realities relate to seeing and savoring Jesus Christ?

It is profoundly wrong to turn the cross into a proof that self-esteem is the root of mental health. If I stand before the love of God and do not feel a healthy, satisfying, freeing joy unless I turn that love into an echo of my self-esteem, then I am like a man who stands before the Grand Canyon and feels no satisfying wonder until he translates the canyon into a case for his own significance. That is not the presence of mental health, but bondage to self.

The cure for this bondage is to see that God is the one being in the universe for whom self-exaltation is the most loving act. In exalting himself—Grand Canyon-like—he gets the glory and we get the joy. The greatest news in all the world is that there is no final conflict between my passion for joy and God's passion for his glory. The knot that ties these together is the truth that God is most glorified in us when we are most satisfied in him. Jesus Christ died and rose again to forgive the treason of our souls, which have turned from savoring God to savoring self. In the cross of Christ, God rescues us from the house of mirrors and leads us out to the mountains and canyons of his majesty. Nothing satisfies us—or magnifies him—more.[6]

FURTHER UP AND FURTHER IN

REFLECTION #1: THE WISDOM OF JESUS CHRIST

Meditate on the following biblical texts in your own Bible:

- Matthew 11:25-27
- John 2:23-25
- John 13:12-19
- Matthew 12:38-42

Read Chapter 6, "Something Greater Than Solomon Is Here," in *Seeing and Savoring Jesus Christ*.

REFLECTION #2: THE DESECRATION OF JESUS CHRIST
Meditate on the following biblical texts in your own Bible:

> ❯ Mark 3:20-30   ❯ Matthew 27:38-44
> ❯ Matthew 11:16-19   ❯ 1 Peter 2:21-25

Read Chapter 7, "The Glorious Poverty of a Bad Reputation," in *Seeing and Savoring Jesus Christ*.

WHILE YOU WATCH THE DVD, TAKE NOTES
What is the first reason that John Piper gives for why seeing and savoring Jesus Christ is so important?

Saving faith is a _____. It is not a _____, _____ or _____.

What are the two components of saving faith that John Piper mentions?

What is the second reason that John Piper gives for why seeing and savoring Jesus Christ is so important?

What two examples does John Piper provide in order to illustrate that we were made for majesty?

AFTER YOU WATCH THE DVD, DISCUSS WHAT YOU'VE LEARNED

1) Discuss whether or not saving faith includes receiving Jesus Christ as infinitely valuable. Do you agree that genuine faith must include savoring Christ above all things?

2) Why is it crucial for us to preach that saving faith includes a supreme delight in the value of Jesus Christ?

What dangers lie in store for us if we don't preach this way?

3) Discuss the evidence that suggests that human beings were made for majesty. What other examples can you think of?

AFTER YOU DISCUSS, MAKE APPLICATION

1) What was the most meaningful part of this lesson for you? Was there a sentence, concept, or idea that really struck you? Why? Record your thoughts in the space below.

2) This week ask two people (preferably non-Christians) why they think people are drawn to the Grand Canyon and other natural wonders. Ask them why admiring

greatness is so enjoyable to everyone. Record their answers below.

NOTES

1. Excerpt taken from *When I Don't Desire God*, pages 34-35.
2. Excerpt taken from *God Is the Gospel*, page 84.
3. Excerpt taken from an online article at the Desiring God web site entitled, "Emphasis in Our Teaching."
4. Excerpt taken from *God Is the Gospel*, pages 37-38.
5. Excerpt taken from an online sermon at the Desiring God web site entitled, "Christ Is Hallowed in Us When We Hope in Him."
6. Excerpt taken from an online article at the Desiring God web site entitled, "The Goal of God's Love May Not Be What You Think It Is."

LESSON 5
THE DIVERSE EXCELLENCIES OF JESUS CHRIST
A Companion Study to the Seeing and Savoring Jesus Christ DVD, Session 4

LESSON OBJECTIVES
It is our prayer that after you have finished this lesson . . .

> You will begin to marvel at the variety of glories that are found in Jesus Christ.

> You will glorify Jesus for his lion-like supremacy.

> You will glorify Jesus for his lamb-like humility.

BEFORE YOU WATCH THE DVD, STUDY AND PREPARE

DAY 1: DIVERSE EXCELLENCIES
In the following lessons, we will begin to look at different qualities and attributes of Jesus Christ. Our examination will in no way be exhaustive. Instead, you will be introduced to some of the diverse excellencies of the Son of God. Our hope is that this introduction will set you on a lifelong endeavor to see and savor more of Jesus Christ.

We will begin with a discussion of music. In the following quotation, John Piper contends that the beauty of harmony is greater and richer than the beauty of melody.

> There is a different kind of unity enjoyed by the joining of diverse counterparts than is enjoyed by joining two things just alike. When we all sing the same melody line, it is called "unison," which means "one sound." But when we unite diverse lines of soprano and alto and tenor and bass, we call it harmony, and everyone who has an ear to hear knows that something deeper in us is touched by great harmony than by unison.[1]

QUESTION 1: Interact with this quotation. Is it true that there is "something deeper" about harmony as opposed to unison? What other analogies would illustrate the same point?

> What I am trying to express here is that the glory of Christ, as he appeared among us, consisted not in one attribute or another, and not in one act or another, but in what Jonathan Edwards called "an admirable conjunction of diverse excellencies." . . . In other words,
>
> › we admire him for his glory, but even more because his glory is mingled with humility;
>
> › we admire him for his transcendence, but even more because his transcendence is accompanied by condescension;

❯ we admire him for his uncompromising justice, but even more because it is tempered with mercy;

❯ we admire him for his majesty, but even more because it is a majesty in meekness;

❯ we admire him because of his equality with his God, but even more because as God's equal he nevertheless has a deep reverence for God;

❯ we admire him because of how worthy he was of all good, but even more because this was accompanied by an amazing patience to suffer evil;

❯ we admire him because of his sovereign dominion over the world, but even more because this dominion was clothed with a spirit of obedience and submission;

❯ we love the way he stumped the proud scribes with his wisdom, and we love it even more because he could be simple enough to like children and spend time with them;

❯ and we admire him because he could still the storm, but even more because he refused to use that power to strike the Samaritans with lightning (Luke 9:54-55) and he refused to use it to get himself down from the cross.[2]

QUESTION 2: How would you demonstrate to another person that "diverse excellencies" are more admirable than one-dimensional excellencies?

DAY 2: THE LION OF JUDAH

We cannot fully see and savor Jesus Christ until we understand the promises of his coming in the Old Testament.

Study Genesis 49:9-10, Isaiah 11:1-4, 10, Jeremiah 23:5-6, and Daniel 7:13-14.

GENESIS 49:9-10

9 Judah is a lion's cub; from the prey, my son, you have gone up. He stooped down; he crouched as a lion and as a lioness; who dares rouse him? 10 The scepter shall not depart from Judah, nor the ruler's staff from between his feet, until tribute comes to him; and to him shall be the obedience of the peoples.

ISAIAH 11:1-4, 10

1 There shall come forth a shoot from the stump of Jesse, and a branch from his roots shall bear fruit. 2 And the Spirit of the LORD shall rest upon him, the Spirit of wisdom and understanding, the Spirit of counsel and might, the Spirit of knowledge and the fear of the LORD. 3 And his delight shall be in the fear of the LORD. He shall not judge by what his eyes see, or decide disputes by what his ears hear, 4 but with righteousness he shall judge the poor, and decide with equity for the meek of the earth; and he shall strike the earth with the rod of his mouth, and with the breath of his lips he shall kill the wicked. . . . 10 In that day the root of Jesse, who shall stand as a signal for the peoples— of him shall the nations inquire, and his resting place shall be glorious.

JEREMIAH 23:5-6

5 Behold, the days are coming, declares the LORD, when I will raise up for David a righteous Branch, and he shall reign as king and deal wisely, and shall execute justice and righteousness in the land. 6 In his days Judah will be saved, and Israel will dwell securely. And this is the name by which he will be called: "The LORD is our righteousness."

DANIEL 7:13-14

13 I saw in the night visions, and behold, with the clouds of heaven there came one like a son of man, and he came to the Ancient of Days and was presented before him. 14 And to him was given dominion and glory and a kingdom, that all peoples, nations, and languages should serve him; his dominion is an everlasting dominion, which shall not pass away, and his kingdom one that shall not be destroyed.

QUESTION 3: From these passages, summarize what you learned about the Messiah in terms of his origin and in terms of his attributes and role.

Now study the following passage.

REVELATION 5:1-5

1 Then I saw in the right hand of him who was seated on the throne a scroll written within and on the back, sealed with seven seals. 2 And I saw a strong angel proclaiming with a loud voice, "Who is worthy to open the scroll and break its seals?" 3 And no one in heaven or on earth or under the earth was able to open the scroll or to look into it, 4 and I began to weep loudly because no one was found worthy to open the scroll or to look into it. 5 And one of the elders said to me, "Weep no more; behold, the Lion of the tribe of Judah, the Root of David, has conquered, so that he can open the scroll and its seven seals."

QUESTION 4: Compare this passage to the passages from the Old Testament in question 3. What similarities do you notice? What attributes or qualities of Jesus Christ are highlighted in this passage?

DAY 3: THE LAMB WHO WAS SLAIN

The last section emphasized the strength and power of Jesus Christ. This kingly dominion is infinitely admirable. As John Piper says, "God loves the strength of the Lion of Judah. This is why he is worthy in God's eyes to open the scrolls of history and unfold the last days. But the picture is not complete. How did the Lion conquer?"[3]

Read the following passage.

REVELATION 5:5-10

[5] *And one of the elders said to me, "Weep no more; behold, the Lion of the tribe of Judah, the Root of David, has conquered, so that he can open the scroll and its seven seals."* [6] *And between the throne and the four living creatures and among the elders I saw a Lamb standing, as though it had been slain, with seven horns and with seven eyes, which are the seven spirits of God sent out into all the earth.* [7] *And he went and took the scroll from the right hand of him who was seated on the throne.* [8] *And when he had taken the scroll, the four living creatures and the twenty-four elders fell down before the Lamb, each holding a harp, and golden bowls full of incense, which are the prayers of the saints.* [9] *And they sang a new song, saying, "Worthy are*

you to take the scroll and to open its seals, for you were slain, and by your blood you ransomed people for God from every tribe and language and people and nation, [10] and you have made them a kingdom and priests to our God, and they shall reign on the earth."

QUESTION 5: What is so shocking about what John sees between the throne and the elders? In light of this passage, how did the Lion of Judah conquer? How did he become worthy to open the scroll?

Revelation 5 is not the only place in the book where Jesus Christ is called the Lamb.

Read Revelation 6:12-17 and Revelation 17:12-14.

REVELATION 6:12-17

[12] When he opened the sixth seal, I looked, and behold, there was a great earthquake, and the sun became black as sackcloth, the full moon became like blood, [13] and the stars of the sky fell to the earth as the fig tree sheds its winter fruit when shaken by a gale. [14] The sky vanished like a scroll that is being rolled up, and every mountain and island was removed from its place. [15] Then the kings of the earth and the great ones and the generals and the rich and the powerful, and everyone, slave and free, hid themselves in the caves and among the rocks of the mountains, [16] calling to the mountains and rocks, "Fall on us and hide us from the face of him who is seated on the throne, and from the wrath of the Lamb, [17] for the great day of their wrath has come, and who can stand?"

REVELATION 17:12-14

12 And the ten horns that you saw are ten kings who have not yet received royal power, but they are to receive authority as kings for one hour, together with the beast. 13 These are of one mind, and they hand over their power and authority to the beast. 14 They will make war on the Lamb, and the Lamb will conquer them, for he is Lord of lords and King of kings, and those with him are called and chosen and faithful.

QUESTION 6: What is significant about the Lamb in these two passages? How do they reinforce what you saw about the Lamb in Revelation 5? How do these passages shape the way that you view Jesus Christ?

The Lion of Judah conquered because he was willing to act the part of a lamb. He came into Jerusalem on Palm Sunday like a king on the way to a throne, and he went out of Jerusalem on Good Friday like a lamb on the way to the slaughter. He drove out the robbers from the Temple like a lion devouring its prey. And then at the end of the week he gave his majestic neck to the knife, and they slaughtered the Lion of Judah like a sacrificial lamb. . . .

So Christ is a lamb-like Lion and a lion-like Lamb. That is his glory—"an admirable conjunction of diverse excellencies."[4]

DAY 4: THE LAMB-LIKE LION AND OUR DEEPEST LONGINGS

Jesus Christ is the Creator of everything that exists. "For by him all things were created, in heaven and on earth, visible and invisible, whether thrones or dominions or rulers or authorities—all things were created through him and for him" (Colossians 1:16). One of the implications of this truth is that our deepest longings find their deepest satisfaction in seeing and savoring him.

QUESTION 7: Take a moment to reflect on your own deepest longings. What longings do you have that correspond to the reality that Jesus Christ is a humble Lamb?

> This glorious conjunction shines all the brighter because it corresponds perfectly with our personal weariness. . . . Jesus said, "Come to me, all who labor and are heavy laden, and I will give you rest. Take my yoke upon you, and learn from me, for I am gentle and lowly in heart" (Matthew 11:28-29). The lamb-like gentleness and humility of this Lion woos us in our weariness. And we love him for it. If he only recruited like the Marines, who want strength, we would despair of coming.[5]

QUESTION 8: Reflect again on your deepest longings. What longings correspond to the reality that Jesus Christ is a conquering Lion?

But this quality of meekness alone would not be glorious. The gentleness and humility of the lamb-like Lion become brilliant alongside the limitless and everlasting authority of the lion-like Lamb. Only this fits our longing for greatness. Yes, we are weak and weary and heavy-laden. But there burns in every heart, at least from time to time, a dream that our lives will count for something great. To this dream Jesus said, "All authority in heaven and on earth has been given to me. Go therefore and make disciples of all nations. . . . And behold, I am with you always, even to the end of the age" (Matthew 28:18-20).

The lion-like Lamb calls us to take heart from his absolute authority over all reality. And he reminds us that, in all authority, he will be with us to the end of the age. This is what we long for—a champion, an invincible leader. We mere mortals are not simple either. We are pitiful, yet we have mighty passions. We are weak, yet we dream of doing wonders. We are transient, but eternity is written on our hearts. The glory of Christ shines all the brighter because the conjunction of his diverse excellencies corresponds perfectly to our complexity.[6]

DAY 5: HUMBLY OBEDIENT AND HIGHLY EXALTED

Examine the following passage.

PHILIPPIANS 2:5-11

> [5] *Have this mind among yourselves, which is yours in Christ Jesus,* [6] *who, though he was in the form of God, did not count equality with God a thing to be grasped,* [7] *but made himself nothing, taking the form of a servant, being born in the likeness of men.* [8] *And being found in human form, he humbled himself by becoming obedient to the point of death, even death on a*

cross. ⁹ Therefore God has highly exalted him and bestowed on him the name that is above every name, ¹⁰ so that at the name of Jesus every knee should bow, in heaven and on earth and under the earth, ¹¹ and every tongue confess that Jesus Christ is Lord, to the glory of God the Father.

QUESTION 9: How does this passage celebrate the lamb-like humility of Jesus? How does this passage celebrate the lion-like supremacy of Jesus? Record your reflections below.

Now look at the following passage.

PHILIPPIANS 2:1-11

¹ So if there is any encouragement in Christ, any comfort from love, any participation in the Spirit, any affection and sympathy, ² complete my joy by being of the same mind, having the same love, being in full accord and of one mind. ³ Do nothing from rivalry or conceit, but in humility count others more significant than yourselves. ⁴ Let each of you look not only to his own interests, but also to the interests of others. ⁵ Have this mind among yourselves, which is yours in Christ Jesus, ⁶ who, though he was in the form of God, did not count equality with God a thing to be grasped, ⁷ but made himself nothing, taking the form of a servant, being born in the likeness of men. ⁸ And being found in human form, he humbled himself by becoming obedient to the point of death, even death on a cross. ⁹ Therefore God has highly exalted him and bestowed on him the name that is above every name, ¹⁰ so that at the name of Jesus every knee should bow, in heaven and on earth and under the earth, ¹¹ and every tongue confess that Jesus Christ is Lord, to the glory of God the Father.

QUESTION 10: In light of Christ's lamb-like humility and lion-like supremacy, what implications does Paul draw out for us? How should Christ's diverse excellencies affect the way that we live?

FURTHER UP AND FURTHER IN

REFLECTION #1: THE ANGUISH OF JESUS CHRIST
Meditate on the following biblical texts in your own Bible:
> - Matthew 26:36-27:50
> - Luke 22:39-23:46
> - Mark 14:32-15:37
> - John 18:1-19:30

Read Chapter 8, "The Incomparable Sufferings," in *Seeing and Savoring Jesus Christ.*

REFLECTION #2: THE SAVING SACRIFICE OF JESUS CHRIST
Meditate on the following biblical texts in your own Bible:
> - 1 John 3:7-9
> - Hebrews 2:14-15
> - Colossians 2:13-15
> - 1 Corinthians 15:55-57

Read Chapter 9, "The Glory of Rescuing Sinners, Not Removing Satan," in *Seeing and Savoring Jesus Christ.*

WHILE YOU WATCH THE DVD, TAKE NOTES

What conclusion does John Piper draw from his discussion of manhood and womanhood?

What fact does John Piper highlight about Jesus' entrance into Jerusalem on Palm Sunday?

According to John Piper, why isn't the Lamb in Revelation 5 slumping?

What point does John Piper draw from his discussion of Revelation 5?

List three of the paradoxical combinations that John Piper mentions.

1) _____ and _____
2) _____ and _____
3) _____ and _____

AFTER YOU WATCH THE DVD, DISCUSS WHAT YOU'VE LEARNED

1) John Piper argued that having a complex personality is more admirable than a one-dimensional personality. Do you agree with his assessment? Does complexity and diversity make a person or thing more admirable?

2) How would Jesus Christ be less admirable if he was only a conquering Lion and not a humble Lamb? How would he be less admirable if he was only a humble Lamb and not a conquering Lion?

3) Discuss other biblical stories that demonstrate that Christ is a lion-like Lamb and a lamb-like Lion.

AFTER YOU DISCUSS, MAKE APPLICATION

1) What was the most meaningful part of this lesson for you? Was there a sentence, concept, or idea that really struck you? Why? Record your thoughts in the space below.

2) Memorize Philippians 2:6-11 this week. Spend at least ten minutes meditating on the humility and supremacy of Jesus Christ. How should this paradoxical combination affect your life this week? Record your reflections below.

NOTES

1. Excerpt taken from an online article at the Desiring God web site entitled, "Marriage: A Matrix of Christian Hedonism."
2. Excerpt taken from *God Is the Gospel*, pages 52-53.
3. Excerpt taken from *The Pleasures of God*, pages 29-30.
4. Excerpt taken from *Seeing and Savoring Jesus Christ*, pages 30-31.
5. Excerpt taken from *Seeing and Savoring Jesus Christ*, page 31.
6. Excerpt taken from *Seeing and Savoring Jesus Christ*, pages 31-32.

LESSON 6

JESUS CHRIST: SOVEREIGN AND SUBMISSIVE

A Companion Study to the Seeing and Savoring Jesus Christ DVD, Session 5

LESSON OBJECTIVES

It is our prayer that after you have finished this lesson . . .

> You will embrace the truth that Jesus Christ is an infinitely happy Savior.

> You will clearly see that Christ's happiness is more wonderful because it is mingled with sorrow and pain.

> You will marvel at the sovereign submission of the King of kings.

BEFORE YOU WATCH THE DVD, STUDY AND PREPARE

DAY 1: JESUS: HAPPY OR SAD?

Jesus Christ is not only the Son of God, the second person of the Trinity. He is also fully human. As a human being, he experienced the full range of human emotions. But did certain emotions predominate? Was Jesus mainly happy or mainly gloomy?

QUESTION 1: Based upon your reading of the Bible, is Jesus Christ a happy Savior or a sullen Savior? Cite Scripture in your answer.

Study John 15:11, John 17:13, Matthew 25:23, Luke 10:21-22, and Psalm 37:4.

JOHN 15:11

These things I have spoken to you, that my joy may be in you, and that your joy may be full.

JOHN 17:13

But now I am coming to you, and these things I speak in the world, that they may have my joy fulfilled in themselves.

MATTHEW 25:23

His master said to him, "Well done, good and faithful servant. You have been faithful over a little; I will set you over much. Enter into the joy of your master."

LUKE 10:21-22

21 In that same hour he rejoiced in the Holy Spirit and said, "I thank you, Father, Lord of heaven and earth, that you have hidden these things from the wise and understanding and revealed them to little children; yes, Father, for such was your gracious will. 22 All things have been handed over to me by my Father, and no one knows who the Son is except the Father, or who the Father is except the Son and anyone to whom the Son chooses to reveal him."

PSALM 37:4

Delight yourself in the LORD, and he will give you the desires of your heart.

QUESTION 2: Summarize the teaching of these passages. Why do you think Jesus is so full of joy?

It is not glorious to be gloomy. Therefore Christ has never been gloomy. From eternity he has been the mirror of God's infinite mirth. The Wisdom of God spoke these words in Proverbs 8:30, "Then I was beside him, like a master workman, and I was daily his delight, rejoicing before him always." The eternal Christ, God's happy and equal agent in creation, was ever rejoicing before God and ever God's delight. Twice more we see this in the New Testament.

In Hebrews 1:8-9 God speaks to the Son, not to the angels, with these astonishing words: "Your throne, O God, is forever and ever. . . . You have loved righteousness and hated wickedness; therefore God, your God, has anointed you with the oil of *gladness* beyond your companions." Jesus Christ is the happiest being in the universe. His gladness is greater than all the angelic gladness of heaven. He mirrors perfectly the infinite, holy, indomitable mirth of his Father.

Again, in Acts 2:25-31 Peter interprets Psalm 16 to refer to Christ: "'I saw the Lord always before me, for he is at my right hand that I may not be shaken; therefore my heart was *glad*, and my tongue *rejoiced*. . . . For you will not abandon my soul to Hades, or let your Holy One see corruption . . . you will make me full of *gladness* with your presence.'" The risen Christ will shake off the shades of death and be glad with the very gladness of God. The glory of Christ is his infinite, eternal, indestructible gladness in the presence of God.[1]

DAY 2: MAN OF SORROWS

In the last section, you saw that Jesus Christ is indeed a happy Savior. The Son of God is overflowing with indestructible joy. But is he *only* joyful? Or is there a place for sadness in the Savior's life?

Study Isaiah 53:3, Luke 19:41-42, and John 11:33-37.

ISAIAH 53:3

He was despised and rejected by men; a man of sorrows, and acquainted with grief; and as one from whom men hide their faces he was despised, and we esteemed him not.

LUKE 19:41-42

[41] And when he drew near and saw the city, he wept over it, [42] saying, "Would that you, even you, had known on this day the things that make for peace! But now they are hidden from your eyes."

JOHN 11:33-37

> [33] When Jesus saw her weeping, and the Jews who had come
> with her also weeping, he was deeply moved in his spirit and
> greatly troubled. [34] And he said, "Where have you laid him?"
> They said to him, "Lord, come and see." [35] Jesus wept. [36] So the
> Jews said, "See how he loved him!" [37] But some of them said,
> "Could not he who opened the eyes of the blind man also have
> kept this man from dying?"

QUESTION 3: Using these passages, how would you respond
to someone who thought that because Jesus was God he did not
truly experience life as a human being? How do you reconcile these
passages with John Piper's statement that "Christ has never been
gloomy"?

Through the agonies of Gethsemane and Golgotha, Jesus
was sustained by indestructible joy. "For the *joy* that was set
before him [he] endured the cross, despising the shame,
and is seated at the right hand of the throne of God" (Hebrews 12:2). And what was that all-sustaining gladness? It
was the gladness of receiving worship from those he died
to make glad in God. The Good Shepherd rejoices over one
lost sheep (Matthew 18:13). How much more over count-
less armies of the ransomed![2]

QUESTION 4: What lesson should we draw from the fact
that Jesus endured the cross for the joy set before him? How

should we view the intermingling of joy and sorrow in our own lives?

All gracious affections that are a sweet odor to Christ, and that fill the soul of a Christian with a heavenly sweetness and fragrancy, are broken-hearted affections. A truly Christian love, either to God or men, is an humble broken-hearted love. The desires of the saints, however earnest, are humble desires: their hope is an humble hope; and their joy, even when it is unspeakable and full of glory, is an humble, broken-hearted joy, and leaves the Christian more poor in spirit, and more like a little child, and more disposed to an universal lowliness of behavior.[3]

DAY 3: EVEN THE WINDS AND THE WAVES OBEY HIM

Read the following passage.

MARK 4:36-41

36 And leaving the crowd, they took him with them in the boat, just as he was. And other boats were with him. 37 And a great windstorm arose, and the waves were breaking into the boat, so that the boat was already filling. 38 But he was in the stern, asleep on the cushion. And they woke him and said to him, "Teacher, do you not care that we are perishing?" 39 And he awoke and rebuked the wind and said to the sea, "Peace! Be still!" And the wind ceased, and there was a great calm. 40 He said to them, "Why are you so afraid? Have you still no faith?" [41] *And they were filled with great fear and said to one another, "Who then is this, that even the wind and the sea obey him?"*

QUESTION 5: What qualities of Jesus are demonstrated in this story? How should this story comfort us in our afflictions?

The winds and waves are not the only aspects of reality over which Jesus Christ exercises dominion. John Piper describes various areas of life over which God the Father and God the Son reign.

> This "all things" includes the fall of sparrows (Matthew 10:29), the rolling of dice (Proverbs 16:33), the slaughter of his people (Psalm 44:11), the decisions of kings (Proverbs 21:1), the failing of sight (Exodus 4:11), the sickness of children (2 Samuel 12:15), the loss and gain of money (1 Samuel 2:7), the suffering of saints (1 Peter 4:19), the completion of travel plans (James 4:15), the persecution of Christians (Hebrews 12:4-7), the repentance of souls (2 Timothy 2:25), the gift of faith (Philippians 1:29), the pursuit of holiness (Philippians 3:12-13), the growth of believers (Hebrews 6:3), the giving of life and the taking in death (1 Samuel 2:6), and the crucifixion of his Son (Acts 4:27-28).[4]

QUESTION 6: What theological problem is created by the

fact that God reigns over all of these areas with absolute authority? How might you solve this theological problem?

Many Christians are speaking this way about the murderous destruction of the World Trade Towers on September 11, 2001. God did not cause it, but he can use it for good. There are two reasons I do not say this. One is that it goes beyond, and is contrary to, what the Bible teaches. The other is that it undermines the very hope it wants to offer.

First, this statement goes beyond and against the Bible. For some, all they want to say, in denying that God "caused" the calamity, is that God is not a sinner and that God does not remove human accountability and that God is compassionate. That is true—and precious beyond words. But for others, and for most people who hear this slogan, something far more is implied. Namely, God, by his very nature, cannot or would not act to bring about such a calamity. This view of God is what contradicts the Bible and undercuts hope.

How God governs all events in the universe without sinning, and without removing responsibility from man, and with compassionate outcomes is mysterious indeed! But that is what the Bible teaches. God "works all things after the counsel of his will" (Ephesians 1:11). . . .

From the smallest thing to the greatest thing, good and evil, happy and sad, pagan and Christian, pain and pleasure—God governs them all for his wise and just and good purposes (Isaiah 46:10). Lest we miss the point, the Bible speaks most clearly to this in the most painful situations. Amos asks, in time of disaster, "If a calamity occurs in a city has not the LORD done it?" (Amos 3:6). After losing all ten of his children in the collapse of his son's house, Job says, "The LORD gave and the LORD has taken away. Blessed be the name of the LORD" (Job 1:21). After being covered with boils he says, "Shall we indeed accept good from God and not accept adversity?" (Job 2:10). . . .

The other reason I don't say, "God did not cause the calamity, but he can use it for good," is that it undercuts the very hope it wants to create. I ask those who say this: "If you deny that God could have 'used' a million prior events to save 5,000 people from this great evil, what hope then do you have that God could now 'use' this terrible event to save you in the hour of trial?" We say we believe he can use these events for good, but we deny that he could use the events of the past to hold back the evil of September 11. But the Bible teaches he could have restrained this evil (Genesis 20:6). "The LORD nullifies the counsel of the nations; He frustrates the plans of the peoples" (Psalm 33:10). But it was not in his plan to do it. Let us beware. We spare God the burden of his sovereignty and lose our only hope.[5]

DAY 4: WHO KILLED JESUS?

Like much of what you have studied in these lessons, the answer to the question "Who killed Jesus?" is not simple.

Examine the following passage.

ACTS 4:24-28

24 And when they heard it, they lifted their voices together to God and said, "Sovereign Lord, who made the heaven and the earth and the sea and everything in them, [25] *who through the mouth of our father David, your servant, said by the Holy Spirit, 'Why did the Gentiles rage, and the peoples plot in vain?* [26] *The kings of the earth set themselves, and the rulers were gathered together, against the Lord and against his Anointed'—* [27] *for truly in this city there were gathered together against your holy servant Jesus, whom you anointed, both Herod and Pontius Pilate, along with the Gentiles and the peoples of Israel,* [28] *to do whatever your hand and your plan had predestined to take place."*

QUESTION 7: In light of this passage, answer the following questions:

> ❯ Was the death of Jesus planned by God?
> ❯ Underline everyone who was involved in the death of Jesus.
> ❯ Was it evil for these men to put him to death?
> ❯ Did God plan for an evil event to happen?

The betrayal of Jesus by Judas was a morally evil act inspired immediately by Satan (Luke 22:3). . . . The betrayal was sin, and it involved the instrumentality of Satan; but it was part of God's ordained plan. That is, there is a sense in which God willed the delivering up of his Son, even though the act was sin.

Moreover, Herod's contempt for Jesus (Luke 23:11), Pilate's spineless expediency (Luke 23:24), the Jewish crowd's cry, "Crucify, crucify him!" (Luke 23:21), and the Gentile soldiers' mockery (Luke 23:36) were also sinful attitudes and deeds.

Yet in Acts 4:27-28 Luke expresses his understanding of the sovereignty of God in these acts by recording the prayer of the Jerusalem saints. . . . Herod, Pilate, the soldiers, and Jewish crowds lifted up their hand to rebel against the Most High, only to find that their rebellion was unwitting (sinful) service in the inscrutable designs of God.[6]

Study Luke 13:31-33 and John 10:17-18.

LUKE 13:31-33

31 At that very hour some Pharisees came and said to him, "Get away from here, for Herod wants to kill you." 32 And he said to them, "Go and tell that fox, 'Behold, I cast out demons and perform cures today and tomorrow, and the third day I finish my course. 33 Nevertheless, I must go on my way today and tomorrow and the day following, for it cannot be that a prophet should perish away from Jerusalem.'"

JOHN 10:17-18

17 For this reason the Father loves me, because I lay down my life that I may take it up again. 18 No one takes it from me, but I lay it down of my own accord. I have authority to lay it down, and I have authority to take it up again. This charge I have received from my Father.

QUESTION 8: How do these texts demonstrate the absolute sovereignty of Jesus? In light of this, how would you respond to someone who said, "The crucifixion of Christ frustrated God's plan"?

DAY 5: SOVEREIGN AND SUBMISSIVE

Many people stumble over the truth presented in the previous section. They do not understand how God can ordain that sinful events occur and yet not be the author of evil. Reconciling God's absolute sovereignty over evil with man's full responsibility for evil is beyond the scope of this study guide.[7] Instead, our main burden is that you recognize and embrace that the Bible clearly teaches that Jesus Christ reigns over all of reality, including evil, and that human beings are fully responsible for their actions. This truth is illustrated in many different places in the Bible.[8] The crucifixion of Christ is simply one of the clearest examples.

QUESTION 9: What is your reaction to the biblical teaching that Jesus Christ is sovereign over all things, including suffering and evil? How does the fact that Christ joyfully submitted to the plan of God that included his own agonizing death make him more admirable?

I conclude, therefore, that God permitted Satan's fall, not because he was helpless to stop it, but because he had a purpose for it. Since God is never taken off guard, his permissions are always purposeful. If he chooses to permit something, he does so for a reason—an infinitely wise reason. How the sin arises in Satan's heart, we do not know. God has not told us. What we do know is that God is sovereign over Satan, and therefore Satan's will does not move without God's permission. And therefore every move

SEEING AND SAVORING JESUS CHRIST

of Satan is part of God's overall purpose and plan. And this is true in such a way that God never sins. God is infinitely holy, and God is infinitely mighty. Satan is evil, and Satan is under the all-governing wisdom of God.[9]

QUESTION 10: In light of what you've learned in this lesson, how would you seek to comfort and encourage someone who is enduring suffering and affliction? What would you want them to see about Jesus?

Following the terrorist attacks of September 11, John Piper wrote a short article entitled "How Shall We Minister to People After the World Trade Tower Terrorism of September 11, 2001?" The following are a few of the points that he made.

1. Pray. Ask God for his help for you and for those you want to minister to. Ask him for wisdom and compassion and strength and a word fitly chosen. Ask that those who are suffering would look to God as their help and hope and healing and strength. Ask that he would make your mouth a fountain of life. . . .

2. Feel and express empathy with those most hurt by this great evil and loss; weep with those who weep. . . .

3. Feel and express compassion because of the tragic circumstances of so many loved ones and friends who have lost more than they could ever estimate. . . .

5. Hold out the promise that God will sustain and help those who cast themselves on him for mercy and trust in his grace. He will strengthen you for the impossible days ahead in spite of all darkness. . . .

9. Express the truth that Satan is a massive reality in the universe that conspires with our own sin and flesh and the world to hurt people and to move people to hurt others, but stress that Satan is within and under the control of God. . . .

14. Mingle heart-wrenching weeping with unbreakable confidence in the goodness and sovereignty of God who rules over and through the sin and the plans of rebellious people. . . .

15. Trust God for his ability to do the humanly impossible, and bring you through this nightmare and, in some inscrutable way, bring good out of it. . . .

18. Count God your only lasting treasure, because he is the only sure and stable thing in the universe. . . .

FURTHER UP AND FURTHER IN

REFLECTION #1: THE MERCIES OF JESUS CHRIST

Meditate on the following biblical texts in your own Bible:

- › Ephesians 2:1-10
- › Romans 15:8-9
- › Luke 18:35-43
- › Mark 1:39-42
- › Luke 15

Read Chapter 10, "The Incarnate Wealth of the Compassion of God," in *Seeing and Savoring Jesus Christ*.

REFLECTION #2: THE SEVERITY OF JESUS CHRIST
Meditate on the following biblical texts in your own Bible:

- Matthew 23
- Luke 14:25-33
- Luke 12:49-53
- Matthew 7:13-14
- Revelation 1:12-16
- Revelation 19:11-16

Read Chapter 11, "The Tough Side," in *Seeing and Savoring Jesus Christ*.

WHILE YOU WATCH THE DVD, TAKE NOTES

What theological problem is created by Jesus' calming the storm?

According to John Piper, what is one of God's purposes for permitting natural disasters and calamities? What text does he draw this purpose from?

What lesson does John Piper draw from Jesus' words to Peter?

What image does John Piper use to illustrate the meaning of "This is your hour, and the power of darkness"?

Any _____ _____ can _____. Jesus didn't _____. That's why I love him.

AFTER YOU WATCH THE DVD, DISCUSS WHAT YOU'VE LEARNED

1) Discuss the complexity of Jesus' affections. How does his indestructible joy lead you to worship him? How does the depth of his sorrow lead you to admire him? What would be lost if Jesus wasn't joyful? What would be lost if Jesus didn't experience pain and sadness?

2) Reflect on the sovereignty of Jesus over all things. How does Christ's sovereignty provide a firm rock for us to

stand on when adversity comes? What questions do you still have about the sovereignty of Christ?

3) Why is it so important to affirm both the sovereignty and the submission of Christ? What is lost if we only embrace the truth that Christ is sovereign over all things? What is lost if we only embrace the truth that Christ endured horrible evil in submission to God's plan?

AFTER YOU DISCUSS, MAKE APPLICATION

1) What was the most meaningful part of this lesson for you? Was there a sentence, concept, or idea that really struck you? Why? Record your thoughts in the space below.

2) Reflect on a time in your life when God allowed you to endure suffering that he could have prevented. Why do you think God allowed you to undergo this adversity? In hindsight, was it good and wise for God to send this suffering into your life? Record your reflections below.

NOTES

1. Excerpt taken from *Seeing and Savoring Jesus Christ*, pages 36-37.
2. Excerpt taken from *Seeing and Savoring Jesus Christ*, page 38.
3. Excerpt is a quotation of Jonathan Edwards taken from an online sermon at the Desiring God web site entitled, "Fear Not, You Worm Jacob!"
4. Excerpt taken from an online article at the Desiring God web site entitled, "Why I Do Not Say 'God Did Not Cause This Calamity, But He Can Use It for Good.'"
5. Excerpt taken from an online article at the Desiring God web site entitled, "Why I Do Not Say 'God Did Not Cause This Calamity, But He Can Use It for Good.'"
6. Excerpt taken from an online article at the Desiring God web site entitled, "Are There Two Wills in God?"
7. For further study in this area, see the Sovereignty of God section in the Topic Index of the Resource Library at the Desiring God web site.
8. For other examples of God's sovereignty over human and demonic evil, see the story of Joseph in Genesis 37-50, the story of Job (particularly Job 1-2), and the story of Pharaoh in Exodus 3-14.
9. Excerpt taken from an online sermon at the Desiring God web site entitled, "The Fall of Satan and the Victory of Christ."

LESSON 7
IS FOLLOWING JESUS SAFE OR DANGEROUS?
A Companion Study to the Seeing and Savoring Jesus Christ DVD, Session 6

LESSON OBJECTIVES

It is our prayer that after you have finished this lesson . . .

> You will be strengthened to follow Jesus on the narrow way that leads to life.

> You will begin to fight and labor to be more dependent upon Jesus.

> You will be stunned by the absolute authority and the comforting presence of Jesus Christ.

BEFORE YOU WATCH THE DVD, STUDY AND PREPARE

DAY 1: AN EASY YOKE OR A NARROW WAY?

QUESTION 1: If someone asked you, "Is it easy or hard to follow Jesus?" how would you answer? What Scriptures would you use to answer this question?

As with many of the paradoxical combinations that you have studied, the answer to the question above is not simple.

Read Matthew 7:13-14 and Matthew 11:28-30.

MATTHEW 7:13-14

[13] *Enter by the narrow gate. For the gate is wide and the way is easy that leads to destruction, and those who enter by it are many.* [14] *For the gate is narrow and the way is hard that leads to life, and those who find it are few.*

MATTHEW 11:28-30

[28] *Come to me, all who labor and are heavy laden, and I will give you rest.* [29] *Take my yoke upon you, and learn from me, for I am gentle and lowly in heart, and you will find rest for your souls.* [30] *For my yoke is easy, and my burden is light.*

QUESTION 2: Attempt to reconcile these two statements by Jesus. If it is hard to enter by the narrow gate, how can it be easy to bear his burden?

So there they are. The two descriptions of the Christian life: wrestling and rest.

> Strive to enter through the narrow door. Life is war. Fight the good fight. Wrestle.

> Come to me, you who are weary, and rest. Find a light yoke and an easy burden.

How can it be both? . . .

I will give you my short answer. It is both wrestling and resting partly because our hearts do not naturally rest in all that God is for us in Jesus. So we must fight against everything that inclines us to rest in anything but Jesus.[1]

DAY 2: FIGHT LIKE A CHILD?

One of the most shocking aspects of following Jesus is that it turns our understanding of importance and competence on its head. Jesus repeatedly undercuts our notions of greatness.

Read Matthew 18:1-4 and Luke 18:16-17.

MATTHEW 18:1-4

[1] At that time the disciples came to Jesus, saying, "Who is the greatest in the kingdom of heaven?" [2] And calling to him a child, he put him in the midst of them [3] and said, "Truly, I say to you, unless you turn and become like children, you will never enter the kingdom of heaven. [4] Whoever humbles himself like this child is the greatest in the kingdom of heaven."

LUKE 18:16-17

[16] But Jesus called them to him, saying, "Let the children come to me, and do not hinder them, for to such belongs the kingdom

of God. ¹⁷ Truly, I say to you, whoever does not receive the
kingdom of God like a child shall not enter it."

QUESTION 3: In light of these passages, how would you
define faith? Why do we have such a difficult time trusting Christ
like a child?

Children are not the only models of faith for Christians. The
apostle Paul uses other analogies in order to encourage the early
Christians in their faith.

Study 1 Corinthians 9:24-27, 1 Timothy 6:12, 2 Timothy
2:3-6, and 2 Timothy 4:7.

1 CORINTHIANS 9:24-27

²⁴ Do you not know that in a race all the runners run, but only
one receives the prize? So run that you may obtain it. ²⁵ Every
athlete exercises self-control in all things. They do it to receive
a perishable wreath, but we an imperishable. ²⁶ So I do not run
aimlessly; I do not box as one beating the air. ²⁷ But I discipline
my body and keep it under control, lest after preaching to others
I myself should be disqualified.

1 TIMOTHY 6:12

¹² Fight the good fight of the faith. Take hold of the eternal life
to which you were called and about which you made the good
confession in the presence of many witnesses.

2 TIMOTHY 2:3-6

> [3] Share in suffering as a good soldier of Christ Jesus. [4] No soldier gets entangled in civilian pursuits, since his aim is to please the one who enlisted him. [5] An athlete is not crowned unless he competes according to the rules. [6] It is the hard-working farmer who ought to have the first share of the crops.

2 TIMOTHY 4:7

> [7] I have fought the good fight, I have finished the race, I have kept the faith.

QUESTION 4: List each of the analogies that Paul uses in these texts. What aspects of faith are highlighted by these analogies?

Faith is something that must be fought for, if it is to thrive and survive. This is how we take hold on eternal life—by fighting to maintain faith, with its joy in Christ. . . .

Oh, that the church would waken to the warfare we are in and feel the urgency of the fight for joy. This is how we hold fast to eternal life. "Fight the good fight of the faith. Take hold of the eternal life" (1 Tim. 6:12). Faith has in it the taste of joy in the glory of Christ. Therefore the good fight of faith is the fight for joy.[2]

DAY 3: THE DANGERS OF FOLLOWING JESUS

God is a stronghold and a refuge. The Bible tells us that "the name of the LORD is a strong tower; the righteous man runs into it and is safe" (Proverbs 18:10). The psalmist writes of his confidence in God's protection: "In peace I will both lie down and sleep; for you alone, O LORD, make me dwell in safety" (Psalm 4:8). But is this the whole story? Is following Jesus safe or dangerous?

Examine John 16:1-4, Luke 21:12-19, and Luke 9:23-25.

JOHN 16:1-4

¹ I have said all these things to you to keep you from falling away. ² They will put you out of the synagogues. Indeed, the hour is coming when whoever kills you will think he is offering service to God. ³ And they will do these things because they have not known the Father, nor me. ⁴ But I have said these things to you, that when their hour comes you may remember that I told them to you. I did not say these things to you from the beginning, because I was with you.

LUKE 21:12-19

¹⁹ But before all this they will lay their hands on you and persecute you, delivering you up to the synagogues and prisons, and you will be brought before kings and governors for my name's sake. ¹³ This will be your opportunity to bear witness. ¹⁴ Settle it therefore in your minds not to meditate beforehand how to answer, ¹⁵ for I will give you a mouth and wisdom, which none of your adversaries will be able to withstand or contradict. ¹⁶ You will be delivered up even by parents and brothers and relatives and friends, and some of you they will put to death. ¹⁷ You will be hated by all for my name's sake. ¹⁸ But not a hair of your head will perish. ¹⁹ By your endurance you will gain your lives.

LUKE 9:23-25

> *23 And he said to all, "If anyone would come after me, let him deny himself and take up his cross daily and follow me. 24 For whoever would save his life will lose it, but whoever loses his life for my sake will save it. 25 For what does it profit a man if he gains the whole world and loses or forfeits himself?"*

QUESTION 5: In light of these texts, is it safe or dangerous to follow Jesus? What is most shocking to you about these passages? According to Jesus, why will people hate us and kill us?

QUESTION 6: Attempt to reconcile Luke 21:16 with Luke 21:18. If some will be killed, how will not a hair of their head perish?

DAY 4: FEAR NOT!

In the last section, we saw that following Jesus does not guarantee us safety and security. Jesus promises that we will be hated and killed. Words like these naturally produce fear in us. But Jesus is ready with a comforting word.

Study the following passage.

MATTHEW 10:24-30

24 A disciple is not above his teacher, nor a servant above his master. 25 It is enough for the disciple to be like his teacher, and the servant like his master. If they have called the master of the house Beelzebul, how much more will they malign those of his household. 26 So have no fear of them, for nothing is covered that will not be revealed, or hidden that will not be known. 27 What I tell you in the dark, say in the light, and what you hear whispered, proclaim on the housetops. 28 And do not fear those who kill the body but cannot kill the soul. Rather fear him who can destroy both soul and body in hell. 29 Are not two sparrows sold for a penny? And not one of them will fall to the ground apart from your Father. 30 But even the hairs of your head are all numbered.

QUESTION 7: What is shocking about Jesus' command to "have no fear of them" in verse 26? Why should we not fear those who will kill us? Whom should we fear instead? How is this passage a comfort to Christians undergoing persecution?

Read the following passage.

LUKE 14:25-33

25 Now great crowds accompanied him, and he turned and said to them, 26 "If anyone comes to me and does not hate his own father and mother and wife and children and brothers and sisters, yes, and even his own life, he cannot be my disciple. 27 Whoever does not bear his own cross and come after me cannot be my disciple. 28 For which of you, desiring to build a tower, does not first sit down and count the cost, whether he has enough to complete it? 29 Otherwise, when he has laid a foundation and is not able to finish, all who see it begin to mock him, 30 saying, 'This man began to build and was not able to finish.' 31 Or what king, going out to encounter another king in war, will not sit down first and deliberate whether he is able with ten thousand to meet him who comes against him with twenty thousand? 32 And if not, while the other is yet a great way off, he sends a delegation and asks for terms of peace. 33 So therefore, any one of you who does not renounce all that he has cannot be my disciple."

QUESTION 8: What is Jesus' counsel to prospective disciples in this passage? In light of what you've studied in this lesson, why is this good advice? Practically speaking, what does it mean to "count the cost"?

DAY 5: THE PRESENCE OF THE KING

The closing words of the Gospel of Matthew are often called "The Great Commission." This final command from Jesus is filled with power and hope.

Study the following passage.

MATTHEW 28:18-20

18 And Jesus came and said to them, "All authority in heaven and on earth has been given to me. 19 Go therefore and make disciples of all nations, baptizing them in the name of the Father and of the Son and of the Holy Spirit, 20 teaching them to observe all that I have commanded you. And behold, I am with you always, to the end of the age."

QUESTION 9: Underline every obligation that Jesus gives us in this text. Explain why each one is significant.

QUESTION 10: What two promises does Jesus give us in this passage? How do these enable us to fulfill Jesus' command? How do these promises highlight the "diverse excellencies" of Jesus Christ?

FURTHER UP AND FURTHER IN

REFLECTION #1: THE RESURRECTION OF JESUS CHRIST
Meditate on the following biblical texts in your own Bible:
- John 10:17-18
- Luke 13:31-32
- Acts 2:22-36
- Ephesians 1:15-23
- 1 Corinthians 15:20-28

Read Chapter 12, "Invincible Life," in *Seeing and Savoring Jesus Christ*.

REFLECTION #2: THE SECOND COMING OF JESUS CHRIST
Meditate on the following biblical texts in your own Bible:
- Matthew 25:31-46
- 2 Thessalonians 1:5-10
- Hebrews 9:27-28
- 1 John 3:1-2
- Titus 2:11-14

Read Chapter 13, "The Appearing of the Glory of Our Great God and Savior," in *Seeing and Savoring Jesus Christ*.

WHILE YOU WATCH THE DVD, TAKE NOTES

According to John Piper, why does Jesus talk in such confusing and complicated ways?

What illustration does John Piper use to illustrate how the way can be hard but the yoke easy?

According to John Piper, what is the most important text for his philosophy of ministry?

If some of your _____ come back in a _____, you haven't _____.

According to John Piper, what does Jesus mean by "not a hair of your head will perish"?

AFTER YOU WATCH THE DVD, DISCUSS WHAT YOU'VE LEARNED

1) Discuss the reasons why it is so difficult to trust Jesus. What evidence of this difficulty do you see in your own life? How can you overcome this difficulty?

2) In light of what you've learned, how should we think about missionaries seeking to enter countries where sharing the gospel is illegal and dangerous?

3) Should Christians move away from comfort and security toward need and risk? Explain your answer.

AFTER YOU DISCUSS, MAKE APPLICATION

1) What was the most meaningful part of this lesson for you? Was there a sentence, concept, or idea that really struck you? Why? Record your thoughts in the space below.

2) Identify three areas of your life where you have difficulty depending on the Lord like a child. Reflect on what prevents you from entrusting these issues to Jesus. Pray through these issues, and commend them to the Lord.

NOTES

1. Excerpt taken from an online sermon at the Desiring God web site entitled, "Resting and Wrestling for the Cause of Christ—Together."

2. Excerpt taken from *When I Don't Desire God*, pages 37-38.

LESSON 8
REVIEW AND CONCLUSION

LESSON OBJECTIVES

It is our prayer that after you have finished this lesson . . .

> You will be able to summarize and synthesize what you've learned.

> You will hear what others in your group have learned.

> You will share with others how you have begun to see the gospel in a new light.

WHAT HAVE YOU LEARNED?

There are no study questions to answer in preparation for this lesson. Instead, spend your time writing a few paragraphs that explain what you've learned in this group study. To help you do this, you may choose to review the notes you've taken in the previous lessons. Then, after you've written down what you've learned, write down some questions that still remain in your mind about anything addressed in these lessons. Be prepared to share these reflections and questions with the group in the next lesson.

NOTES

Use this space to record anything in the group discussion that you want to remember:

LEADER'S GUIDE

AS THE LEADER OF THIS GROUP STUDY, *it is impera-tive that you are completely familiar with this study guide* and with the *Seeing and Savoring Jesus Christ* DVD Set. Therefore, it is our strong recommendation that you (1) read and understand the introduction, (2) skim each lesson, surveying its layout and content, and (3) read the entire Leader's Guide *before* you begin the group study and distribute the study guides. As you review this Leader's Guide, keep in mind that the material here is only a recommendation. As the leader of the study, feel free to adapt this study guide to your situation and context.

BEFORE LESSON 1

Before the first lesson, you will need to know approximately how many participants you will have in your group study. *Each partici-pant will need his or her own study guide!* Therefore, be sure to order enough study guides. You will distribute these study guides at the beginning of the first lesson.

It is also our strong recommendation that you, as the leader, familiarize yourself with this study guide and the *Seeing and Savoring Jesus Christ* DVD Set in order to answer any questions that might arise and also to ensure that each group session runs smoothly and maximizes the learning of the participants. It is not necessary for you to preview *Seeing and Savoring Jesus Christ* in its entirety—although it certainly wouldn't hurt!—but you should be prepared to navigate your way through each DVD menu.

NOTE: As we noted in the Introduction, this study guide is designed for an eight-session guided study. However, we understand that there are times when a group may only have six weeks with which to complete this study. In such a case, we recommend abbreviating Lesson 1 and completing it along with Lesson 2 in the first week. The preparatory work for Lesson 2 can be completed as a group during the first session. In addition, Lesson 8 may be completed by students on their own after the group has met for the final time.

DURING LESSON 1

Each lesson is designed for a one-hour group session. Lessons 2-8 require preparatory work from the participant before the group session. Lesson 1, however, requires no preparation on the part of the participant.

The following schedule is how we suggest that you use the first hour of your group study:

INTRODUCTION TO THE STUDY GUIDE (10 MINUTES)

Introduce this study guide and the *Seeing and Savoring Jesus Christ* DVD. Share with the group why you chose to lead the group study using these resources. Inform your group of the commitment that this study will require and motivate them to work hard. Pray for the eight-week study, asking God for the grace you will need. Then distribute one study guide to each participant. You may read the introduction aloud, if you want, or you may immediately turn the group to Lesson 1 (starting on page 11 of this study guide).

PERSONAL INTRODUCTIONS (15 MINUTES)

Since group discussion will be an integral part of this guided study, it is crucial that each participant feels welcome and safe. The goal of each lesson is for every participant to contribute to the discussion in some way. Therefore, during these fifteen minutes, have the participants introduce themselves. You may choose to use the questions listed in the section entitled "About Yourself," or you may ask questions of your own choosing.

DISCUSSION (25 MINUTES)

Transition from the time of introductions to the discussion questions, listed under the heading "A Preview of *Seeing and Savoring Jesus Christ*." Invite everyone in the class to respond to these questions, but don't let the discussion become too involved. These questions are designed to spark interest and generate questions. The aim is not to come to definitive answers yet.

REVIEW AND CLOSING (10 MINUTES)

End the group session by reviewing Lesson 1 with the group participants and informing them of the preparation that they must do before the group meets again. Encourage them to be faithful in preparing for the next lesson. Answer any questions that the group may have and then close in prayer.

BEFORE LESSONS 2-8

As the group leader, you should do all the preparation for each lesson that is required of the group participants—that is, the ten study questions. Furthermore, it is highly recommended that you complete the entire "Further Up and Further In" section. This is not required of the group participants, but it will enrich your preparation and will help you guide and shape the conversation more effectively.

The group leader should also preview the session of *Seeing and Savoring Jesus Christ* that will be covered in the next lesson. So, for example, if the group participants are doing the preparatory work for Lesson 3, you should preview *Seeing and Savoring Jesus Christ*, Session 2, before the group meets and views it. Previewing each session will better equip you to understand the material and answer questions. If you want to pause the DVD in the midst of the session in order to clarify or discuss, previewing the session will allow you to plan where you want to take your pauses.

Finally, you may want to supplement or modify the discussion questions or the application assignment. Please remember that *this study guide is a resource*; any additions or changes you make that better match the study to your particular group are encouraged. As the group leader, your own discernment, creativity, and guidance are invaluable, and you should adapt the material as you see fit.

Plan for about two hours of your own preparation before each lesson!

DURING LESSONS 2-7

Again, let us stress that during Lessons 2-7 you may use the group time in whatever way you desire. The following schedule, however, is what we suggest:

DISCUSSION (10 MINUTES)

Begin your time with prayer. The tone you set in your prayer will likely be impressed upon the group participants: if your prayer is serious and heartfelt, the group participants will be serious about prayer; if your prayer is hasty, sloppy, or a token gesture, the group participants will share this same attitude toward prayer. So model the kind of praying that you desire your students to imitate. Remember, the blood of Jesus has bought your access to the throne of grace.

After praying, review the preparatory work that the participants completed. How did they answer the questions? Which questions did they find to be the most interesting or the most confusing? What observations or insights can they share with the group? If you would like to review some tips for leading productive discussion, please turn to the appendix at the end of this book.

The group participants will be provided an opportunity to apply what they've learned in Lessons 2-7. As the group leader, you can choose whether it would be appropriate for the group to discuss these assignments during this ten-minute time-slot.

DVD VIEWING (30 MINUTES)[1]

Play the session of *Seeing and Savoring Jesus Christ* that corresponds to the lesson you're studying. You may choose to pause the DVD at crucial points to check for understanding and provide clarification. Or you may choose to watch the DVD without interruption.

DISCUSSION AND CLOSING (20 MINUTES)

Foster discussion on what was taught during John Piper's session. You may do this by first reviewing the DVD notes (under the heading "While You Watch the DVD, Take Notes") and then proceeding to the discussion questions, listed under the heading "After You Watch the DVD, Discuss What You've Learned." These discussion questions are meant to be springboards that launch the group into further and deeper discussion. Don't feel constrained to cover these questions if the group discussion begins to move in other helpful directions.

Close the time by briefly reviewing the application section and the homework that is expected for the next lesson. Pray and dismiss.

BEFORE LESSON 8

It is important that you encourage the group participants to complete the preparatory work for Lesson 8. This assignment invites the participants to reflect on what they've learned and what remaining questions they still have. As the group leader, this would be a helpful assignment for you to complete as well. In addition, you may want to write down the key concepts of this DVD series that you want the group participants to walk away with.

DURING LESSON 8

The group participants are expected to complete a reflection exercise as part of their preparation for Lesson 8. The bulk of the group time during this last lesson should be focused on reviewing and synthesizing what was learned. Encourage all participants to share some of their recorded thoughts. Attempt to answer any remaining questions that they might have.

To close this last lesson, you might want to spend extended time in prayer. If appropriate, take prayer requests relating to what the participants have learned in these eight weeks, and bring these requests to God.

It would be completely appropriate for you, the group leader, to give a final charge or word of exhortation to end this group study. Speak from your heart and out of the overflow of joy that you have in God.

Please receive our blessing for all of you group leaders who choose to use this study guide:

> The LORD bless you and keep you; the LORD make his face to shine upon you and be gracious to you; the LORD lift up his countenance upon you and give you peace. (Numbers 6:24-26)

NOTES

1. Thirty minutes is only an approximation. Some of the sessions are shorter; some are longer. You may need to budget your group time differently, depending upon which session you are viewing.

APPENDIX
LEADING PRODUCTIVE DISCUSSIONS

Note: This material has been adapted from curricula produced by The Bethlehem Institute (TBI), a ministry of Bethlehem Baptist Church. It is used by permission.

IT IS OUR CONVICTION THAT the best group leaders foster an environment in their group that engages the participants. Most people learn by solving problems or by working through things that provoke curiosity or concern. Therefore, we discourage you from ever "lecturing" for the entire lesson. Although group leaders will constantly shape conversation, clarifying and correcting as needed, they will probably not talk for the majority of the lesson. This study guide is meant to facilitate an investigation into biblical truth—an investigation that is shared by the group leader and the participants. Therefore, we encourage you to adopt the posture of a "fellow-learner" who invites participation from everyone in the group.

It might surprise you how eager people can be to share what they have learned in preparing for each lesson. Therefore, you should invite participation by asking your group participants to share their discoveries. Here are some of our tips on facilitating discussion that is engaging and helpful:

> › Don't be uncomfortable with silence initially. Once the first participant shares his or her response, others will be likely to join in. But if you cut the silence short by prompting them, they are more likely to wait for you to prompt them every time.

> Affirm every answer, if possible, and draw out the participants by asking for clarification. Your aim is to make them feel comfortable sharing their ideas and learning; so be extremely hesitant to shut down a group member's contribution or trump it with your own. This does not mean, however, that you shouldn't correct false ideas—just do it in a spirit of gentleness and love.

> Don't allow a single person, or group of persons, to dominate the discussion. Involve everyone, if possible, and intentionally invite participation from those who are more reserved or hesitant.

> Labor to show the significance of their study. Emphasize the things that the participants could not have learned without doing the homework.

> Avoid talking too much. The group leader should not monopolize the discussion but rather guide and shape it. If the group leader does the majority of the talking, the participants will be less likely to interact and engage, and therefore they will not learn as much. Avoid constantly adding the "definitive last word."

> The group leader should feel the freedom to linger on a topic or question if the group demonstrates interest. The group leader should also pursue digressions that are helpful and relevant. There is a balance to this, however: the group leader *should* attempt to cover the material. So avoid the extreme of constantly wandering off topic, but also avoid the extreme of limiting the conversation in a way that squelches curiosity or learning.

> The group leader's passion, or lack of it, is infectious. Therefore, if you demonstrate little enthusiasm for the material, it is almost inevitable that your participants will likewise be bored. But if you have a genuine excitement for what you are studying, and if you truly think Bible study is worthwhile, then your group will be impacted

positively. Therefore, it is our recommendation that before you come to the group, you spend enough time working through the homework and praying so you can overflow with genuine enthusiasm for the Bible and for God in your group. This point cannot be stressed enough. Delight yourself in God and in his Word!

✸ desiringGod

If you would like to further explore the vision of God and life presented in this book, we at Desiring God would love to serve you. We have hundreds of resources to help you grow in your passion for Jesus Christ and help you spread that passion to others. At our website, desiringGod.org, you'll find almost everything John Piper has written and preached, including more than thirty books. We've made over twenty-five years of his sermons available free online for you to read, listen to, download, and in some cases watch.

In addition, you can access hundreds of articles, listen to our daily internet radio program, find out where John Piper is speaking, learn about our conferences, discover our God-centered children's curricula, and browse our online store. John Piper receives no royalties from the books he writes and no compensation from Desiring God. The funds are all reinvested into our gospel-spreading efforts. DG also has a whatever-you-can-afford policy, designed for individuals with limited discretionary funds. If you'd like more information about this policy, please contact us at the address or phone number below. We exist to help you treasure Jesus Christ and his gospel above all things because he is most glorified in you when you are most satisfied in him. Let us know how we can serve you!

Desiring God
Post Office Box 2901
Minneapolis, Minnesota 55402

888.346.4700
mail@desiringGod.org
www.desiringGod.org

Personal Notes

Personal Notes

Personal Notes

Personal Notes

Personal Notes

Personal Notes

Personal Notes